Contents

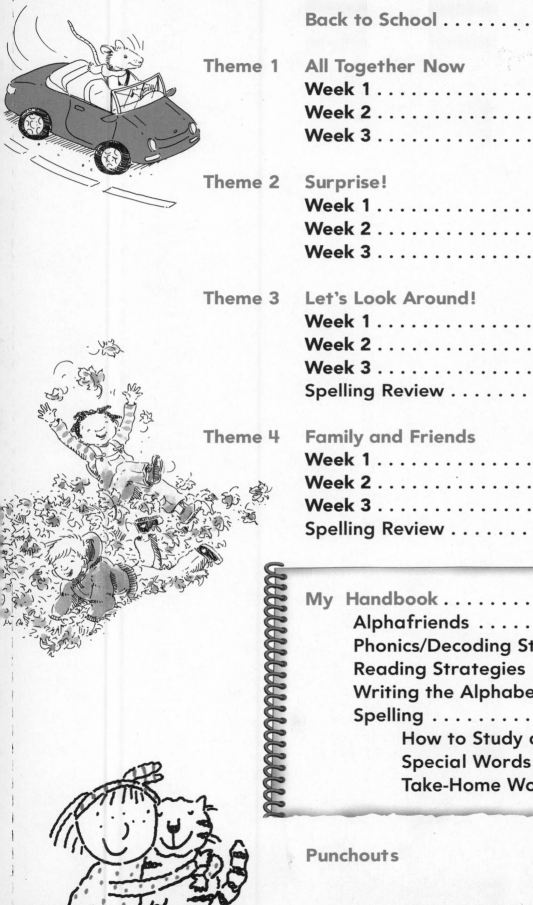

Punchouts

Name _____

What Happened?

The picture shows what happens at the beginning of **My Best Friend.** Draw a picture of something that happens in the middle of the story. Then draw what happens at the end.

Name _____

My Own Best Friend

✏️ Draw a picture of you and your best friend doing something you love to do together.

Name _____

Alphabet Review

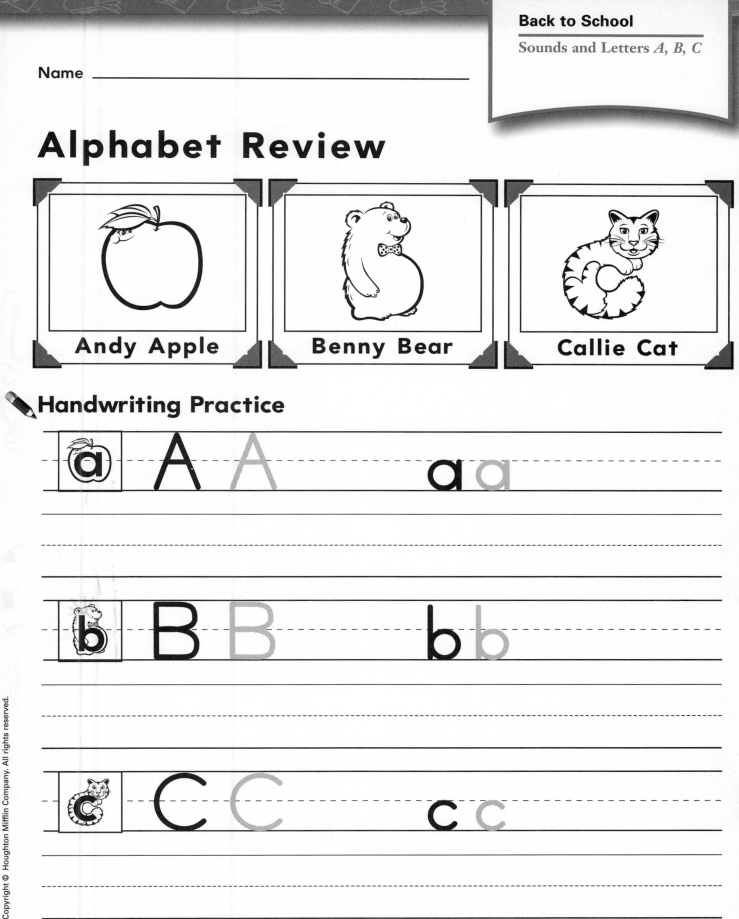

Andy Apple

Benny Bear

Callie Cat

Handwriting Practice

Name _____

Begins with A, B, or C

Phonics Circle the pictures that begin with the letter at the beginning of each row.

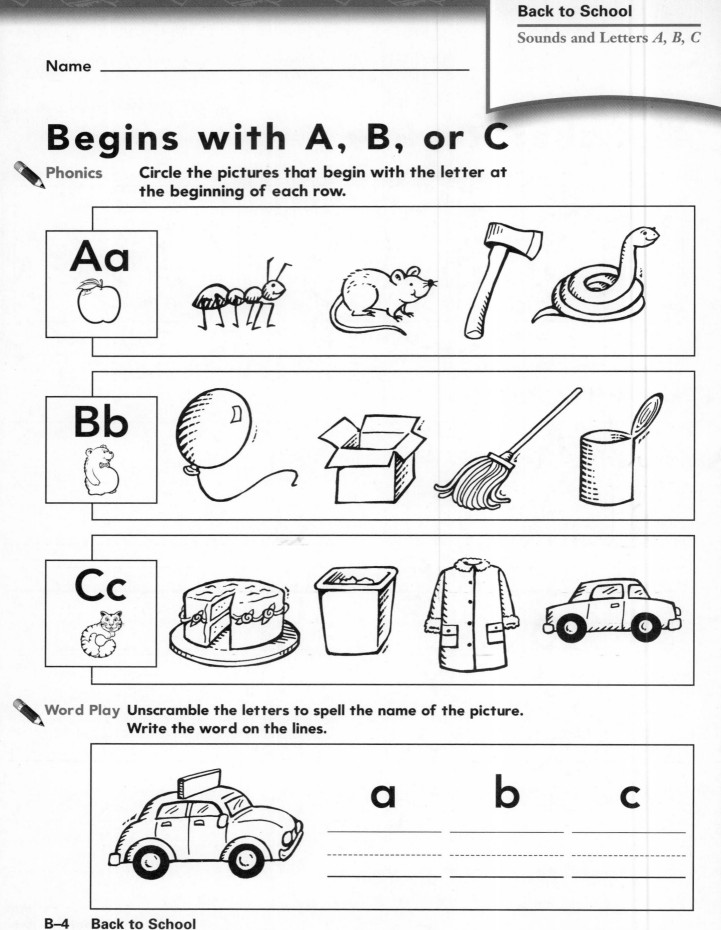

Word Play Unscramble the letters to spell the name of the picture. Write the word on the lines.

a   b   c

Name _____

Alphabet Review

Dudley Duck

Edna Elephant

✏ Handwriting Practice

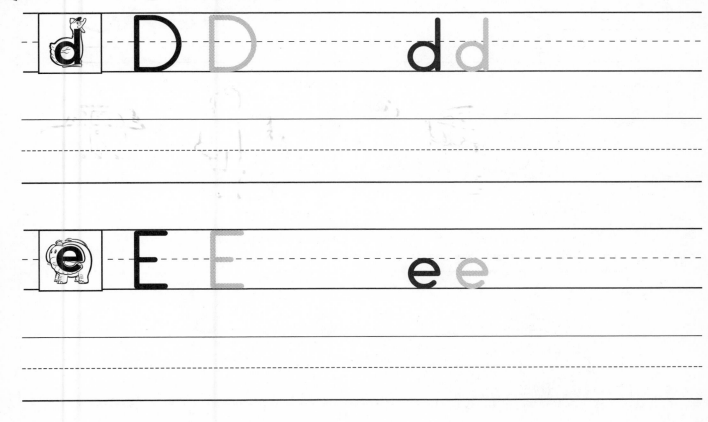

Name _____

Begins with D or E

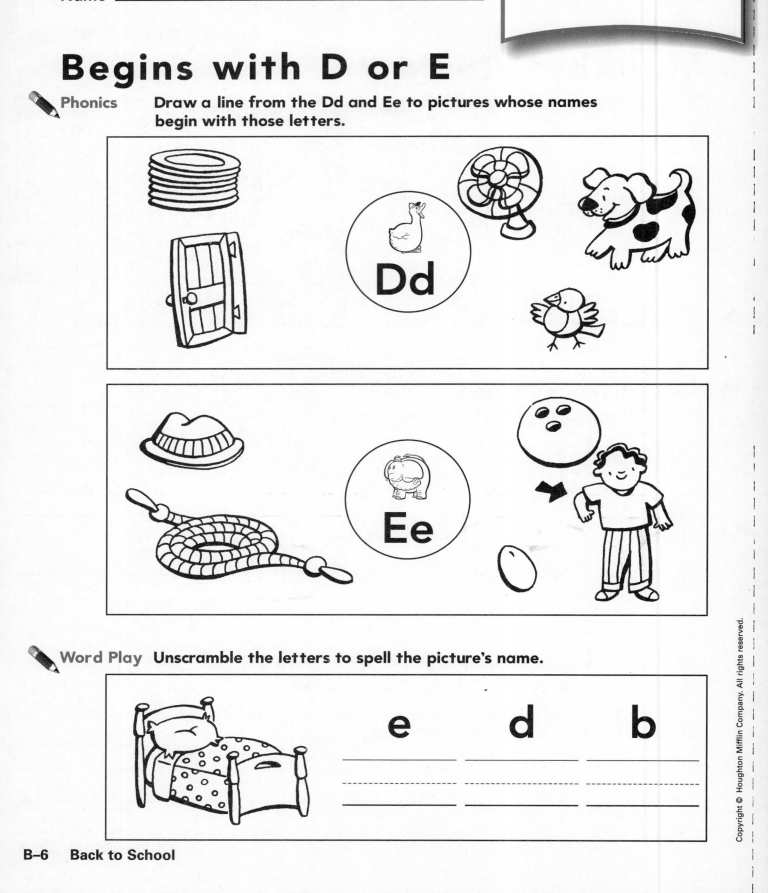

Phonics   Draw a line from the Dd and Ee to pictures whose names begin with those letters.

Word Play   Unscramble the letters to spell the picture's name.

e   d   b

_____ _____ _____

Name _____

Alphabet Review

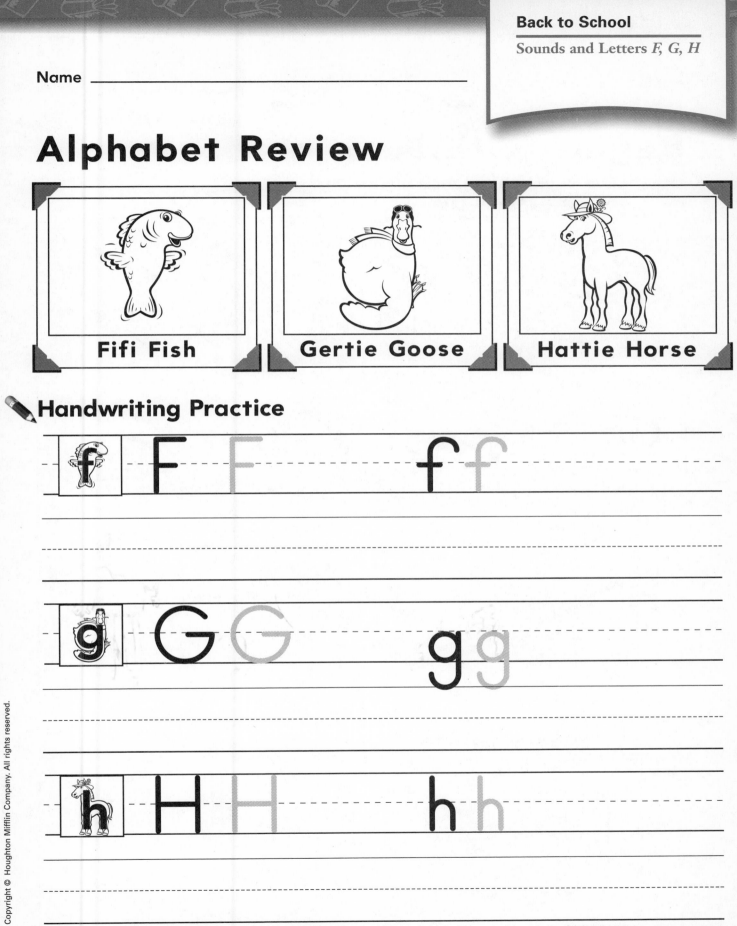

Fifi Fish

Gertie Goose

Hattie Horse

Handwriting Practice

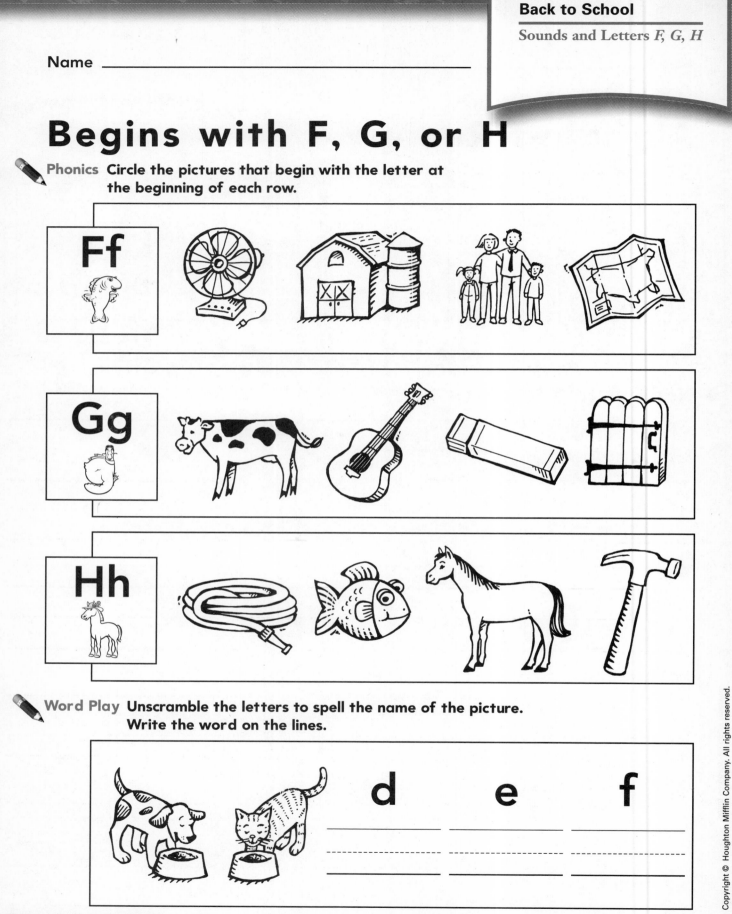

Name _____

Begins with F, G, or H

Phonics Circle the pictures that begin with the letter at the beginning of each row.

Ff

Gg

Hh

Word Play Unscramble the letters to spell the name of the picture. Write the word on the lines.

d   e   f

Name _____

Alphabet Review

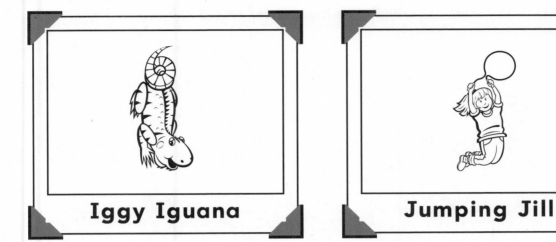

Iggy Iguana   **Jumping Jill**

✏️ Handwriting Practice

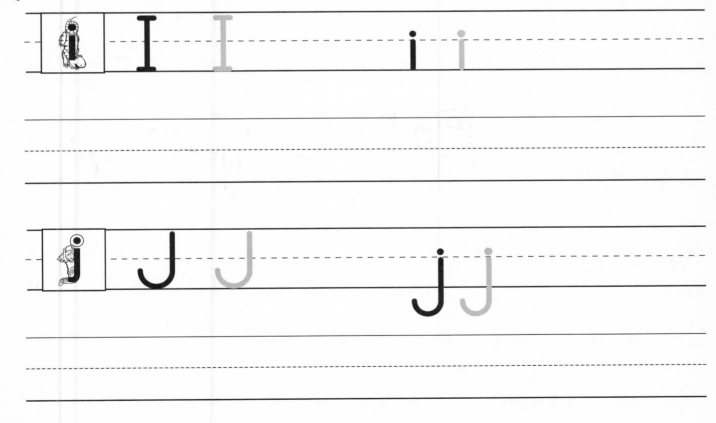

Name _____

Begins with I or J

Phonics Draw a line from the Ii and Jj to the pictures whose names begin with those letters.

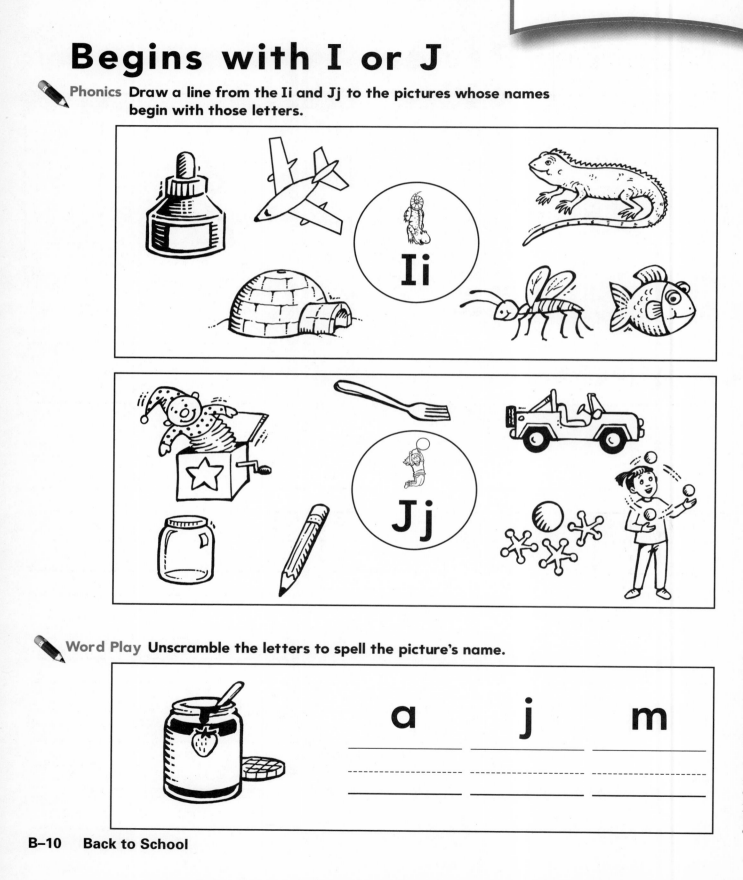

Word Play Unscramble the letters to spell the picture's name.

a   j   m

_____   _____   _____

Name _____

Alphabet Review

Keely Kangaroo   **Larry Lion**   **Mimi Mouse**

✏️ **Handwriting Practice**

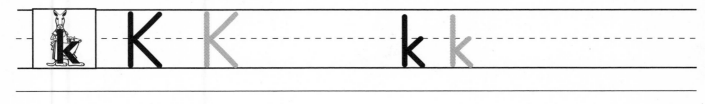

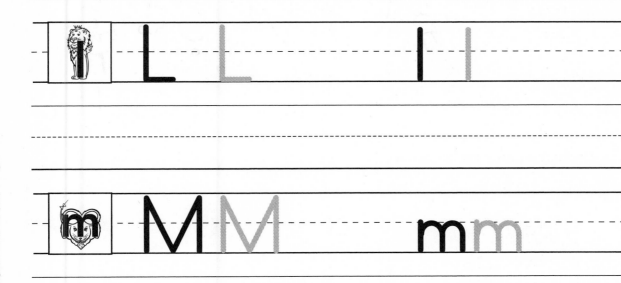

Name _____

Begins with K, L, or M

Phonics Circle the pictures that begin with the letter at the beginning of each row.

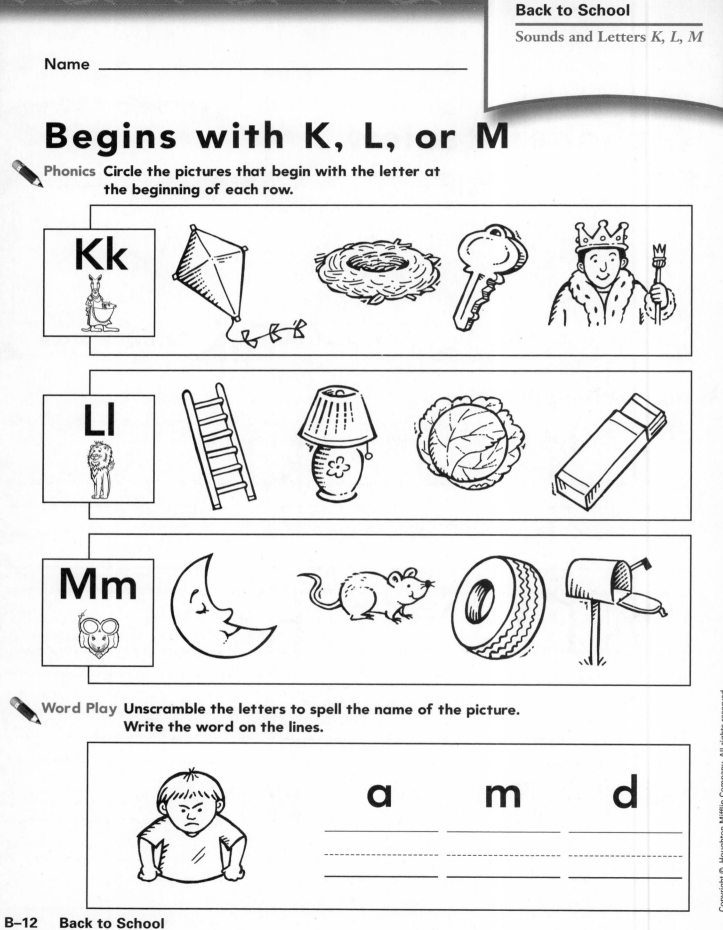

Word Play Unscramble the letters to spell the name of the picture. Write the word on the lines.

a   m   d

Name _____

Alphabet Review

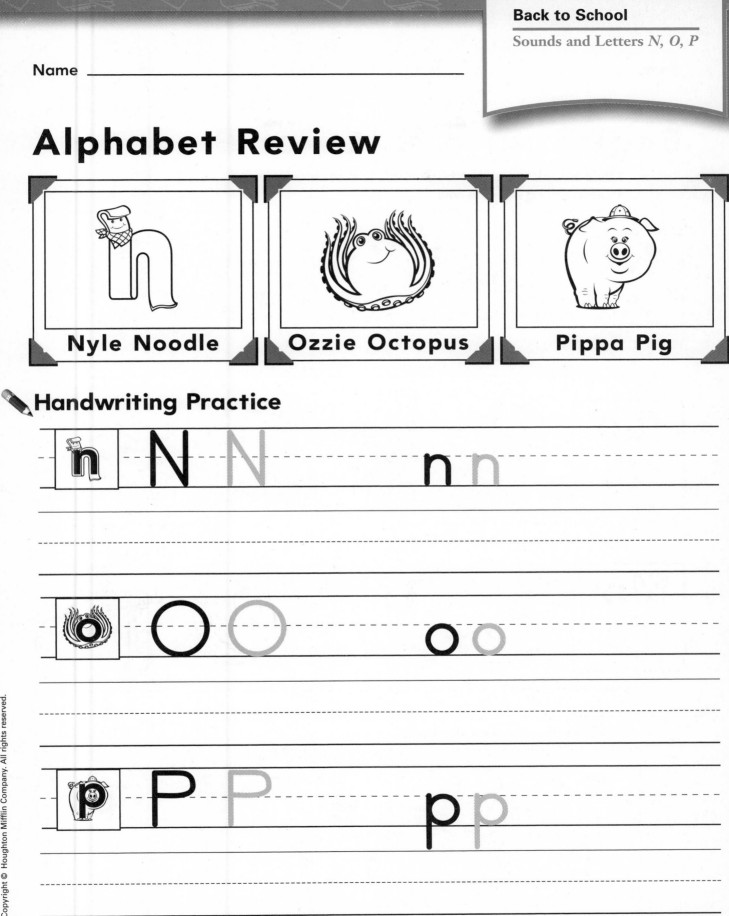

Nyle Noodle   **Ozzie Octopus**   **Pippa Pig**

✏️ **Handwriting Practice**

Name _____

Begins with N, O, or P

Phonics Circle the pictures that begin with the letter at the beginning of each row.

Word Play Unscramble the letters to spell the name of the picture. Write the word on the lines.

g   i   p

Name _____

Alphabet Review

Queenie Queen | **Reggie Rooster** | **Sammy Seal**

 Handwriting Practice

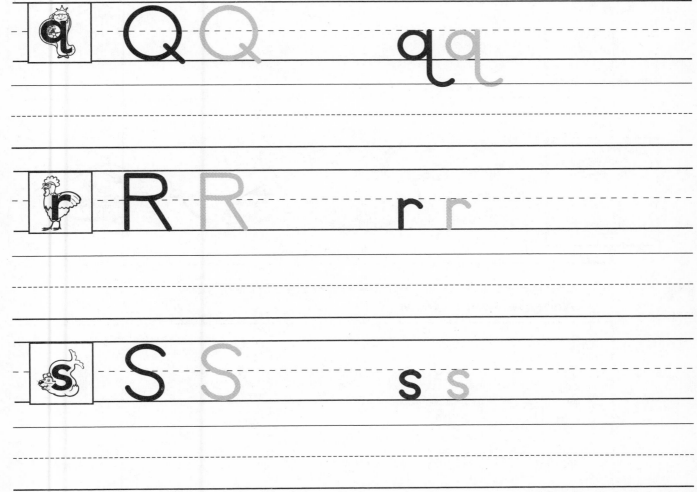

Q Q Q   q q

R R R   r r

S S S   s s

Name _____

Begins with Q, R, or S

Phonics Circle the pictures that begin with the letter at the beginning of each row.

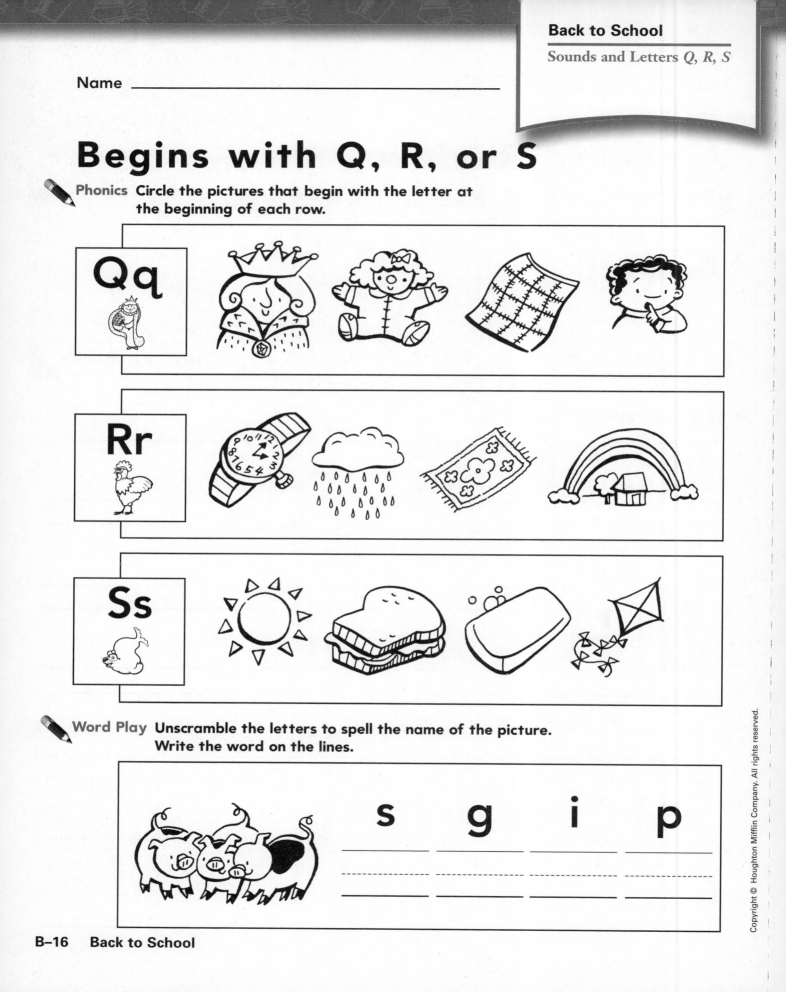

Word Play Unscramble the letters to spell the name of the picture. Write the word on the lines.

s   g   i   p

___ ___ ___ ___

Name _____

Alphabet Review

Tiggy Tiger

Umbie Umbrella

Vinny Volcano

Handwriting Practice

T T T t t

U U U u u

V V V v v

Name _____

Begins with T, U, or V

Phonics Circle the pictures that begin with the letter at the beginning of each row.

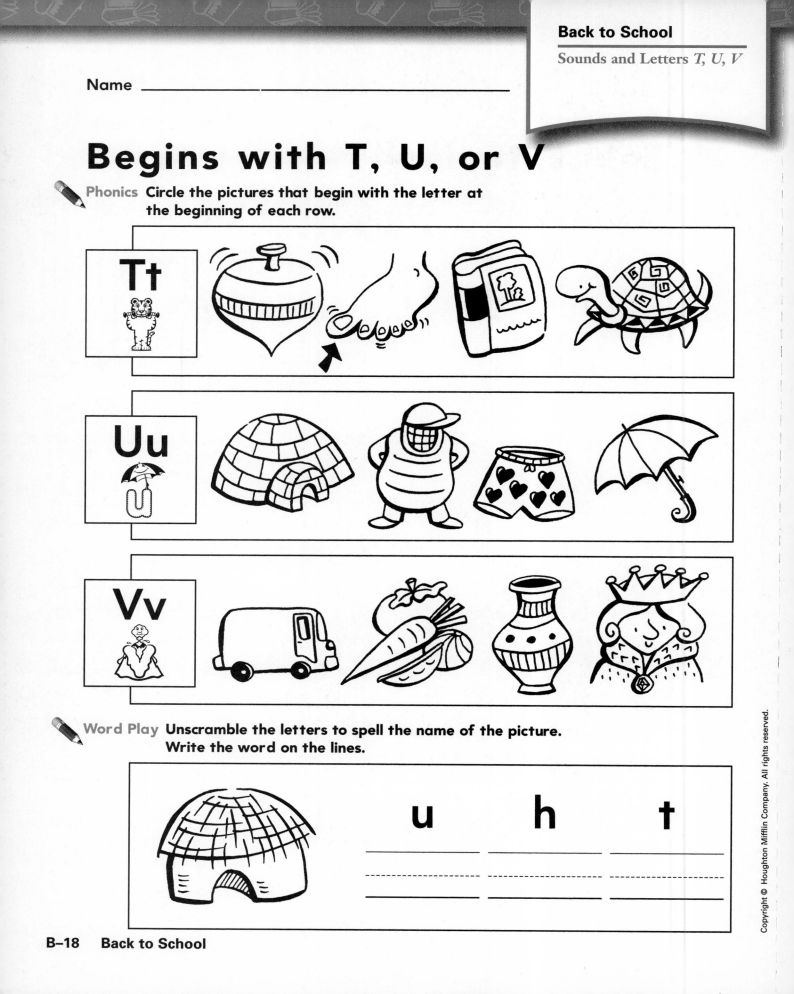

Word Play Unscramble the letters to spell the name of the picture. Write the word on the lines.

u   h   t

_____ _____ _____

Name _____

Alphabet Review

Willy Worm

Mr. X-Ray

✏ Handwriting Practice

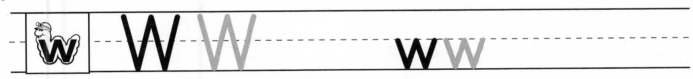

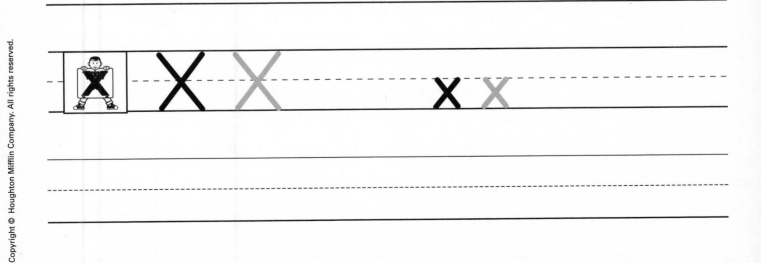

Name _____

Begins with W or X

Phonics Draw a line from the Ww to the pictures whose names
begin with the /hw/ sound.

Ww

Draw a line from the Xx to the pictures whose names
have the /ks/ sound.

Xx

Word Play Unscramble the letters to spell the picture's name.

f   x   o

___ ___ ___

Name _____

Alphabet Review

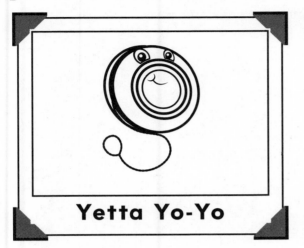

Yetta Yo-Yo

Zelda Zebra

Handwriting Practice

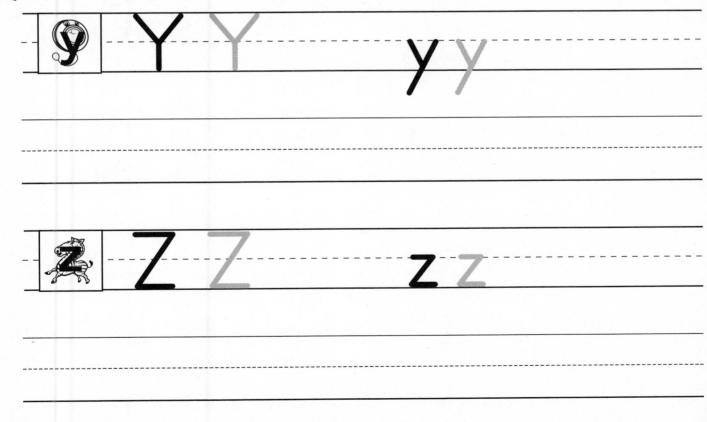

Name _____

Begins with Y or Z

Phonics Draw a line from the Yy and Zz to pictures whose names begin with those letters.

Word Play Unscramble the letters to spell the picture's name.

z g i a g z

___ ___ ___ ___ ___ ___

Name _____

Words with *-at*

✏️ **Write the word next to the correct picture.**

Word Bank

| sat | mat | cat |

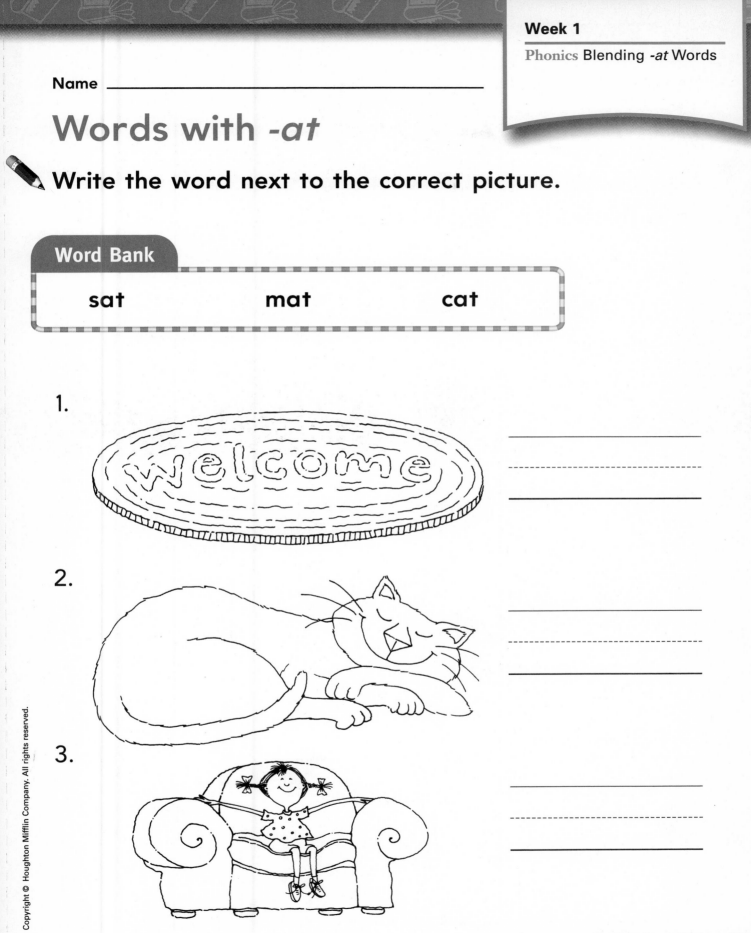

1.

_____

2.

_____

3.

_____

Theme 1: **All Together Now**   **5**

Name _____

Blending *-at* Words

Name each picture. Color the pictures that have the -at sound.

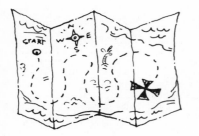

Name _____

Begins with *m* or *s*

Think of each beginning sound.
Write **m** or **s**.

m s

1.

_____

2.

_____

3.

_____

4.

_____

5.

_____

6.

_____

Name _____

Ends with *n*

Name each picture. Color the pictures that have the same ending sound as .

Name _____

Ends with *f*

Name each picture. Color the pictures that
have the same ending sound as  .

Name _____

Ends with *p*

Name each picture. Color the pictures that have the same ending sound as  .

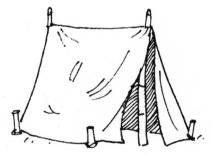

Theme 1: **All Together Now** **21**

Name _____

Words with -an

Blend the sounds for these letters. Then write a word for each picture.

m + an   c + an   p + an   f + an

1.

_____

- - - - - - - - - - - - - -

_____

2.

_____

- - - - - - - - - - - - - -

_____

3.

_____

- - - - - - - - - - - - - -

_____

4.

_____

- - - - - - - - - - - - - -

_____

Words with -*an* and -*at*

Read each word. Look at the picture.

Draw a line to match a word to the picture.

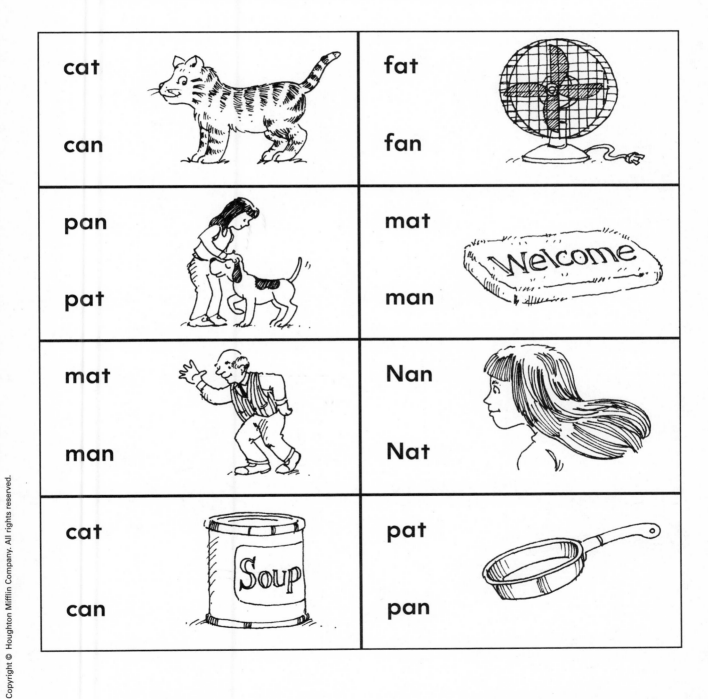

cat		fat	
can		fan	
pan		mat	
pat		man	
mat		Nan	
man		Nat	
cat		pat	
can		pan	

Begins with *n* or *f*

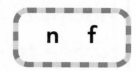

Think of each beginning sound.
Write **n** or **f**.

n   f

1. _____

2. _____

3. _____

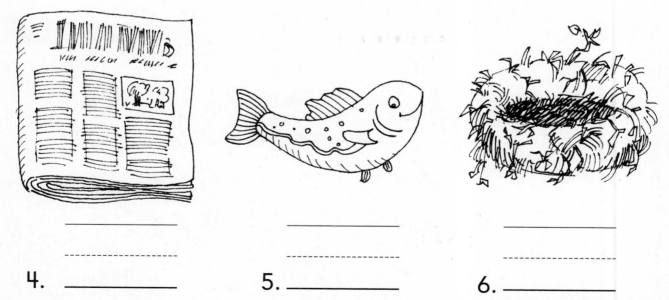

4. _____

5. _____

6. _____

Name _____

What's Different?

Look at both pictures. Put an X on
the things that are different.

Name _seever_

Words to Know

✏ Write a word from the box to match the picture and complete the sentence.

Word Bank

| and | jump | not |

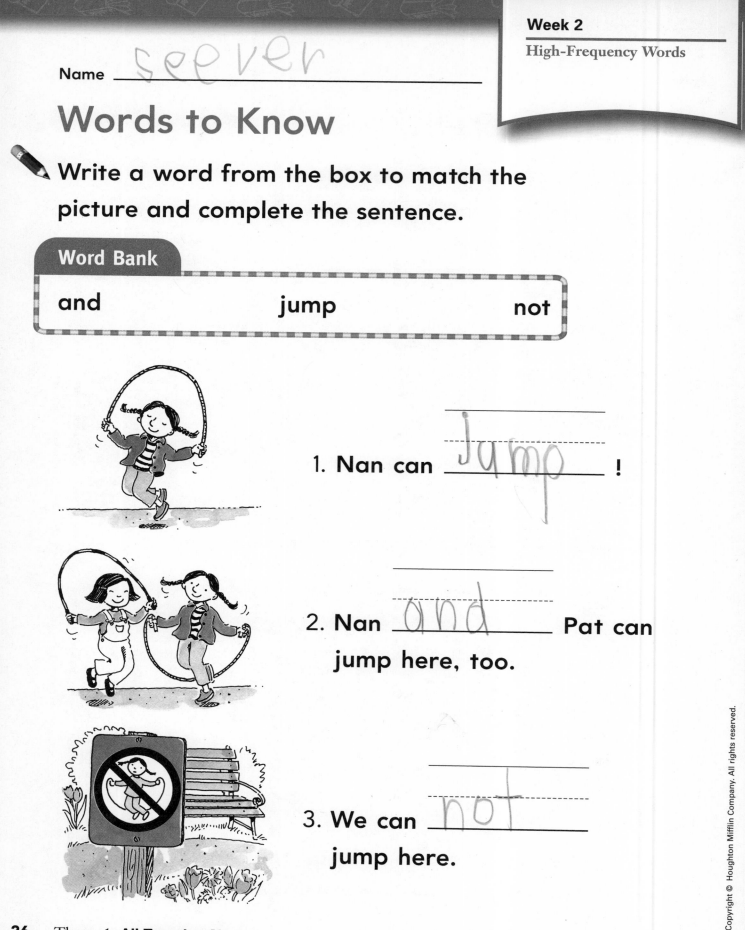

1. Nan can __jump__ !

2. Nan __and__ Pat can jump here, too.

3. We can __not__ jump here.

Name _____

Things We Do at School

Write and draw about something you do
at school.

Cut out your sentence and picture.

Name _____

Begins with *b, g, h, r*

Name each picture. Circle the letter that stands for the beginning sound.

1. b r g

2. h r g

3. b g h

4. r g h

5. b r g

6. b r g

7. h r g

8. b r g

9. b g h

10. r g h

11. b g h

12. b r h

13. b r h

14. b r g

15. b r h

16. r g h

Name _____

Ends with *b*

Name each picture. Color the pictures that
have the same ending sound as  .

Name _____

Ends with g

Name each picture. Color the pictures that have the same ending sound as 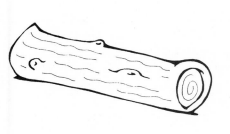.

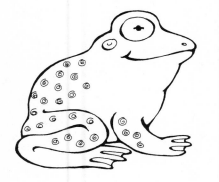

Theme 1: **All Together Now**   **37**

Name _____

Ends with *r*

Name each picture. Color the pictures that have the same ending sound as ⭐ .

Name _____

Words with *-it*

Blend the sounds for these letters. Then write a word for each picture.

| f + it | h + it | p + it | s + it |

1. _____

2. _____

3. _____

4. _____

Name _____

Words with -ig

Blend the sounds for these letters. Then write a word for each picture.

f + ig	b + ig	p + ig

1. _____

2. _____

3. _____

Name _____

Words with -*it* and -*ig*

Read each word. Look at the picture.

Draw a line to match a word to the picture.

pit		fit	
pig		fig	
big		pit	
bit		pig	
bit		sit	
hit		bit	
fit		hit	
fig		bit	

Name _____

Begins with *b* or *h*

Think of each beginning sound.
Write **b** or **h**.

| b   h |

1.

2.

3.

4.

5.

6.

Name _____

What Happened?

Look at each picture. Draw a line from column
A to column B to show why it happened.

A

B

1.

2.

3.

Theme 1: **All Together Now**   43

Name _____

Words to Know

Write a word from the box to match the picture and complete the sentence.

Word Bank

| find | have | Who |

1. Can Pat _____ Nan?

2. We _____ one pig and a cat.

3. _____ can go to the mat?

Name _____

Words to Know

✂ Cut out and paste each sentence next to the
picture it matches.

1.

2.

3.

Who can find the bat?

Who can jump to the hat?

We have one cat and a pig.

Name _____

Begins with *r* or *g*

Think of each beginning sound.
Write **r** or **g**.

r	g

1.

_____

2.

_____

3.

_____

4.

_____

5.

_____

6.

_____

Theme 1: **All Together Now**   **47**

Name _____

Who Can Hit?

Read each sentence. Draw a line from the picture to the sentence that goes with it.

1.

We have a big bat.

Nat can hit.

2.

Go, Nat, go!

Nan can hit, too.

3.

Pat hit a big one.

We ran, ran, ran!

48   Theme 1: **All Together Now**

Name _____

My Own Ending

Write a new ending for **Big Pig.**

_____

- -

_____

- -

_____

- -

_____

- -

_____

Draw a picture to go with your new ending.

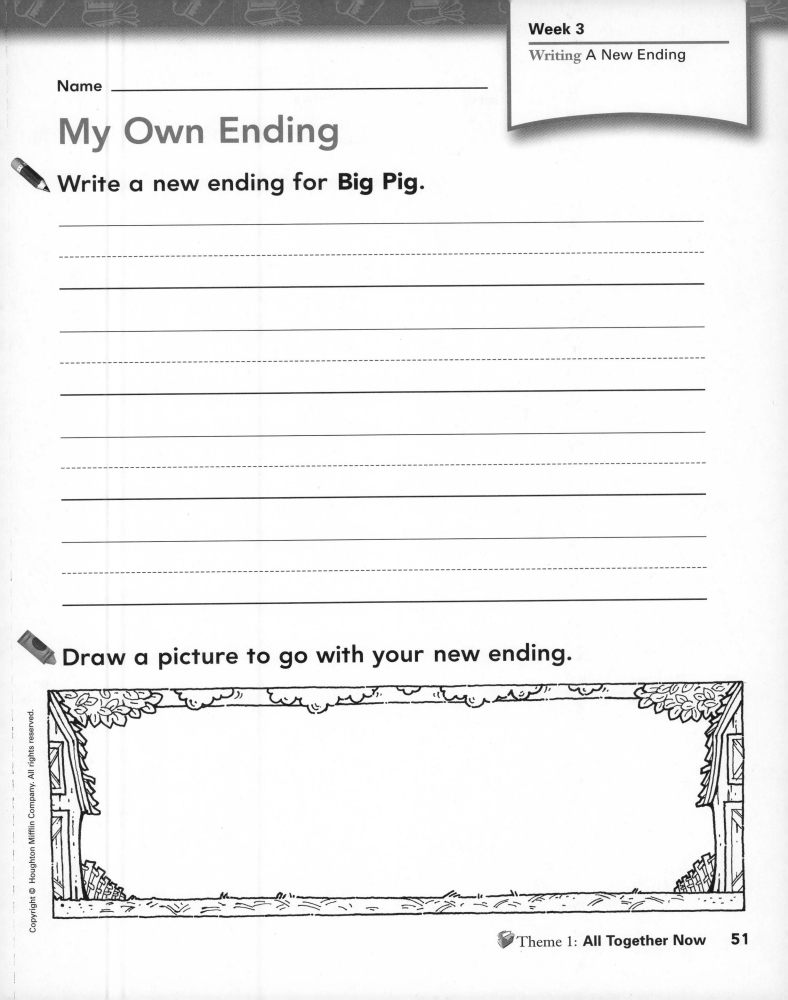

Theme 1: **All Together Now**   **51**

Name _____

Begins with *d, w, l,* or *x*

Name each picture. Circle the letter that stands for the beginning sound.

1. d w l

2. d l x

3. w x d

4. x l d

5. l x w

6. w l d

7. d w l

8. l d w

9. w d l

10. d l w

11. d x w

12. l d w

13. d x l

14. l d w

15. w x d

16. w d l

Ends with *d*

Name each picture. Write **d** if the word ends
like **Ted**. Write **n** if the word ends like **fan**.
Then draw a line from Ted to his bed.
Connect the pictures whose names end like
Ted.

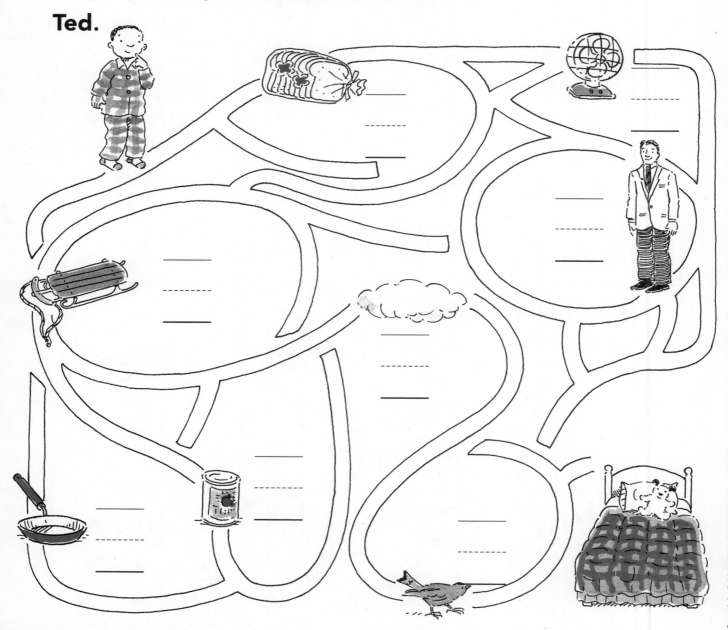

Name _____

Ends with /

Name each picture. Color the pictures that
have the same ending sound as **owl**.

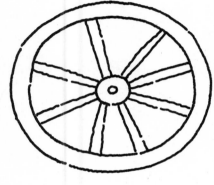  

  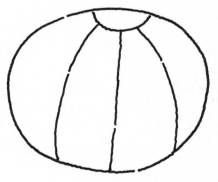

  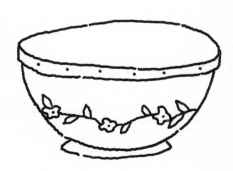

Name _____

Ends with *x*

Name each picture. Write **x** if the word ends
like **mix**. Write **b** if the word ends like **cab**.
Then draw a line from the fox to his box.
Connect the pictures whose names end like **mix**.

Name _____

Words with *-ot*

Blend the sounds for these letters. Then write a word for each picture.

| p + ot | h + ot | c + ot | d + ot |

Name _____

Words with -ox

Complete each sentence with a word from the box.

Word Bank

| ox | fox | box |

1. Go, _____, go!

2. The fox sat on the _____ .

3. The ox sat on the _____ !

Name _____

Words with -*ox* and -*ot*

Read the words in the box. Write a word for each picture.

Word Bank

cot	fox	pot	box	ox	dot

1. _____

2. _____

3. _____

4. _____

5. _____

6. _____

Name _____

Begins with *d* or *l*

Name each picture. Think of the beginning sound. Write **d** or **l**.

d   l

1.	2.	3.
4.	5.	6.
7.	8.	9.
10.	11.	12.

Name _____

Who Can Find It?

Read the sentence. Find that part of the picture, and color it.

Find a cat with one bat.

Find a big hat on an ox.

Theme 2: **Surprise!**   **61**

Name _____

Words to Know

✏️ Draw a line from each story to the picture that matches it.

1. **What have we here?**

   We have one, two, three.

   We have four and five!

2. **A cat can sit.**

   It can sit upon a box.

   It can sit in the box, too.

3. **Can the cat fit in?**

   It fit in the box once.

   The cat got too big!

Name _____

Words to Know

Circle the sentence that matches the picture.

1.

One cat sat upon
a box.

We jump here.

2.

Five sit.

Three have a hat.

3.

A man can bat.

Once, the four fit
in here.

4.

What can we find?

We two have a big
pan.

Theme 2: **Surprise!**   63

Name _____

Begins with *w, x*

✏️ **Name each picture. Circle the pictures that begin with w. Write w if the word begins with w.**

1. _____
_ _ _ _ _ _ _ _ _ _
_____

2. _____
_ _ _ _ _ _ _ _ _ _
_____

3. _____
_ _ _ _ _ _ _ _ _ _
_____

4. _____
_ _ _ _ _ _ _ _ _ _
_____

5. _____
_ _ _ _ _ _ _ _ _ _
_____

6. _____
_ _ _ _ _ _ _ _ _ _
_____

✏️ **Write x to complete each word. Draw a picture for each word.**

fo___

bo___

What's in the Box?

Read each sentence. Draw a line to the picture that goes with the sentence.

1.

2.

3.

4.

5.

6.

A fox can fit in the box.

A pig can fit, too.

A hat can fit in the box.

Dot got the box.

Dan and Dot can fit, too.

Dot can find a lot in the box.

Wigs, Wigs, Wigs!

Read the words in the box. Use the words to finish the sentences.

Word Bank

| ball | Thanks | shelf | win | wigs |

1. What can Nat Cat _____ ?

2. What is on the _____ ?

3. Can Nat Cat win _____ ?

4. Get a _____ , Nat Cat.

5. _____ , Dot Dog!

Name _____

About the Story

Circle the picture that answers each question.

1. Who can hit the ball in?

2. What can Pat Pig win?

3. What can Pat Pig find in the box?

4. Who got the thanks?

Name _____

Lots of Labels

✂ Cut out and paste each word above the
animal whose name begins with the same letter.

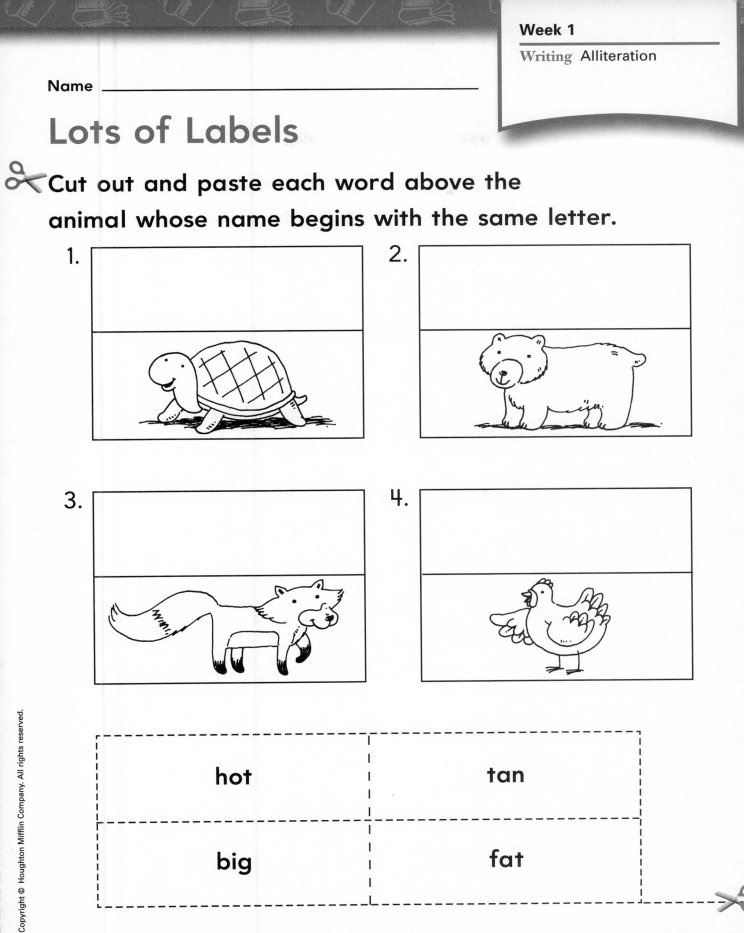

1.

2.

3.

4.

hot

tan

big

fat

Name _____

Words with -en

Blend the sounds for these letters. Then write
a word for each picture.

| m + en | h + en | p + en | t + en |

1. _____

2. _____

3. _____

4. _____

Name _____

The Pet

✏️ Complete each sentence with a word from the box.

Word Bank

| set | pet | let | get |

_____

1. Find a _____ .

_____

2. We can _____ a box.

_____

3. We _____ the pet jump in.

_____

4. We _____ the pet upon the mat.

Name _____

Words with -*et* and -*en*

Read each word. Look at the picture. Draw
a line to match a word to the picture.

pet		met	
pen		men	
bet		pet	
wet		pen	
ten		let	
Ken		hen	
den		vet	
net		yen	

Name _____

Begins with *y* or *v*

✏ **Name each picture. Think of the beginning sound. Write y or v.**

y   v

1.

2.

3.

4.

5.

6.

7.

8.

9.

10.

11.

12.

Name _____

Words to Know

Write words from the box to complete the story.

Word Bank

me	is	said	you

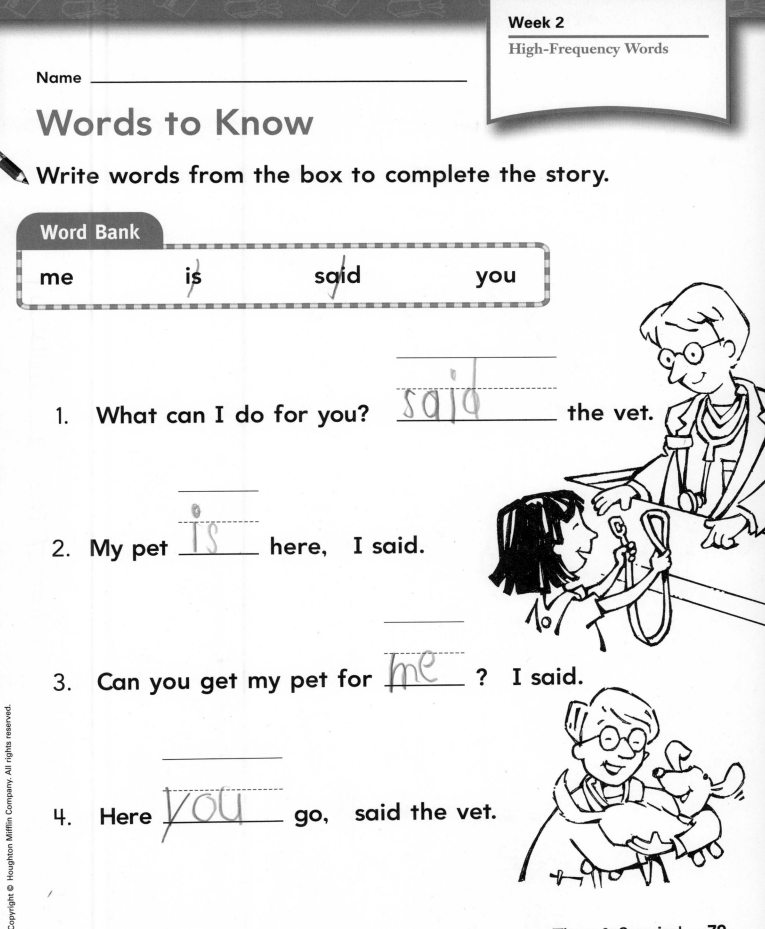

1. What can I do for you? ___said___ the vet.

2. My pet ___is___ here, I said.

3. Can you get my pet for ___me___ ? I said.

4. Here ___you___ go, said the vet.

Name _____

Begins with *k*

Name each picture. Color the pictures that have the same beginning sound as **kit**.

Name _____

Words with -ut

Blend the sounds for these letters. Then write a word for each picture.

h + ut   c + ut   n + ut   r + ut

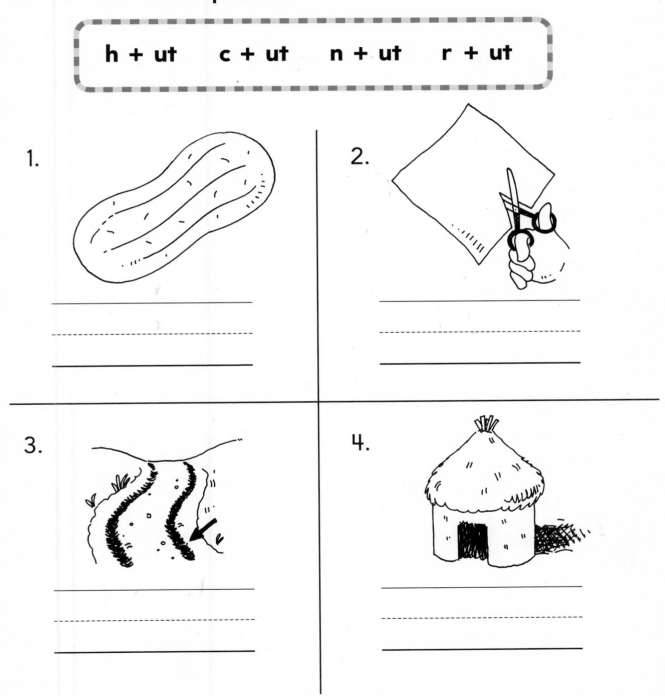

1. _____

2. _____

3. _____

4. _____

Name _____

Words with -*ug*

Blend the sounds for these letters. Then write a word for each picture.

j + ug   m + ug   b + ug   r + ug

1.

_____

2.

_____

3.

_____

4.

_____

Name _____

Words with -*ut* and -*ug*

Read each word. Look at the picture. Draw
a line to match a word to the picture.

jut

jug

rug

rut

bug

but

nut

mug

nut

tug

hug

hut

hug

hut

cut

tug

Name _____

Begins with *j* or *z*

✎ **Name each picture. Think of the beginning sound. Write j or z.**

j   z

1.

2.

3.

4.

5.

6.

7.

8.

9.

10.

11.

12.

Name _____

What a Bug!

Draw a picture of a bug.

Write about the bug.

_____

- -

_____

_____

- -

_____

_____

- -

_____

Name _____

Words with Short *a*

Name each picture. Write a if the picture name has the short a sound.

1.

2.

3.

4.

5.

6.

7.

8.

9.

10.

11.

12.

13.

14.

15.

16.

Theme 3: **Let's Look Around!** **101**

Name _____

Words with Short *a*

Read each sentence and circle the picture of the underlined word. Write the word.

1. What is in the <u>bag</u>?

_____
- - - - - - - - - -
_____

2. We have a <u>yam</u>.

_____
- - - - - - - - - -
_____

3. We have a <u>ham</u>.

_____
- - - - - - - - - -
_____

4. We have <u>jam</u>, too.

_____
- - - - - - - - - -
_____

5. Do you have a <u>pan</u>?

_____
- - - - - - - - - -
_____

102 Theme 3: **Let's Look Around!**

Name _____

More Than One

Read each sentence. Circle the picture of the underlined word.

1. **Where are the animals?**

2. **Ben has cats.**

3. **Nan has hens.**

4. **Kit has a pig.**

Name _____

What's It All About?

Read "Big Cats." Then look at the chart. The topic and main idea are filled in. You add the details. Then use the chart to give a summary.

Big Cats

What can big cats do?

Big cats can jump.

Big cats can sit, too.

Big cats can live in a den.

But big cats are not pets!

Topic	Big Cats
Main Idea	A big cat can do a lot.
Details	

Name _____

The Short *a* Sound

Write a word from the box to finish each sentence.

Spelling Words

an

at

can

cat

had

man

_____
- - - - - - - - - - - - - - - - -
1. My pet is _____ animal.

_____
- - - - - - - - - - - - - - - - -
2. It is a _____ .

_____
- - - - - - - - - - - - - - - - -
3. A _____ let me have the cat.

_____
- - - - - - - - - - - - - - - - -
4. He _____ a lot of cats.

_____
- - - - - - - - - - - - - - - - -
5. My cat _____ do a lot.

_____
- - - - - - - - - - - - - - - - -
6. Look _____ my cat jump!

Theme 3: **Let's Look Around!** 113

Name _____

Make a Sentence

Draw a line from the part of the sentence
that names a person or object to the part
of the sentence that tells what the person or
object can do.

1.    We   can live in a den.

2.   A fox   can live in a hut.

Write the sentences you made.

_____

1. _____

_____

2. _____

_____

Name _____

Spelling Spree

Write the letter for each shape. Make Spelling Words.

an

at

can

cat

had

man

h

n

d

a

m

1. _____

2. _____

3. _____

Proofread each sentence. Circle each Spelling Word that is wrong and write it correctly.

_____

4. I see a big kat. _____

5. Look ad it go! _____

6. It ken jump, too. _____

Name _____

Which Season Is Your Favorite?

✏ Write about your favorite season.

Season _____

_____

_____

_____

_____

_____

_____

_____

_____

Name _____

Words with Short *i*

Name each picture. Write **i** if the picture name has the short **i** sound.

Name _____

Words with Short *i*

Read each sentence and circle the picture of the underlined word. Write the word.

1. Ben is <u>six</u>.

   _____

   - - - - - - - - - - - -

   _____

2. He has a <u>mitt</u>.

   _____

   - - - - - - - - - - - -

   _____

3. The <u>wig</u> is not for Ben.

   _____

   - - - - - - - - - - - -

   _____

4. The <u>bib</u> is not for Ben.

   _____

   - - - - - - - - - - - -

   _____

5. The cap is for <u>him</u>.

   _____

   - - - - - - - - - - - -

   _____

118 Theme 3: **Let's Look Around!**

Name _____

What Happens Next?

✂ **Cut and paste the picture to show what happens next.**

1.

2.

Name _____

Spelling Spree

Write the missing letters. Then write the Spelling Word.

in

it

him

big

sit

did

1. d___d   _____

2. h___m   _____

3. ___t   _____

Proofread each sentence. Circle each Spelling Word that is wrong and write it correctly.

4. The pig is bige.   _____

5. The pig is en a pen!   _____

6. The pig can zit.   _____

Your Favorite Food

✏ **Write sentences to describe your favorite food.**

What is your favorite food?

_____

- - - - - - - - - - - - - - - - - -

_____

- - - - - - - - - - - - - - - - - -

_____

What does it look like?

_____

- - - - - - - - - - - - - - - - - -

_____

- - - - - - - - - - - - - - - - - -

_____

How does it taste?

_____

- - - - - - - - - - - - - - - - - -

_____

- - - - - - - - - - - - - - - - - -

_____

Name _____

Clusters with *r*

Name each picture. Circle the letters that stand for the beginning sounds.

1. cr   pr   fr

2. fr   br   tr

3. br   gr   tr

4. pr   gr   tr

5. br   cr   tr

6. br   dr   fr

7. br   gr   tr

8. cr   dr   tr

9. cr   fr   pr

10. cr   pr   fr

11. br   dr   pr

12. br   fr   pr

13. br   fr   pr

14. cr   pr   fr

15. dr   fr   pr

16. tr   fr   dr

Name _____

Clusters with *r*

✏️ **Circle the word that names each picture.**
Write the word.

1. **brick**   **brim**

    _____

    - - - - - - - - - - - - - - - - -

    _____

2. **grab**   **grass**

    _____

    - - - - - - - - - - - - - - - - -

    _____

3. **drag**   **drip**

    _____

    - - - - - - - - - - - - - - - - -

    _____

4. **crib**   **crab**

    _____

    - - - - - - - - - - - - - - - - -

    _____

5. **trap**   **trip**

    _____

    - - - - - - - - - - - - - - - - -

    _____

6. **crack**   **crab**

    _____

    - - - - - - - - - - - - - - - - -

    _____

Name _____

Words to Know

Read the story. Color the picture that matches the story.

"Look!" said Kris, "I see many animals!"

"Me, too!" said Brad.

Kris said, "I see some green and brown frogs!"

"Me, too!" said Brad.

Kris said, "And I also see a bird as blue as my cap!"

"Me, too," said Brad.

"I like to look at the color of all the pets," said Kris.

"Me, too!" said the bird.

"Funny bird!" said Brad.

Name _____

Words to Know

Write the words that name colors on the fish. Write all the other words on the boat.

Word Bank

also
blue
brown
color
funny
green
like
many
some

Name _____

Words to Know

Write a word from the box to complete each sentence. Use the pictures to help you.

Word Bank

change

fish

sea

whales

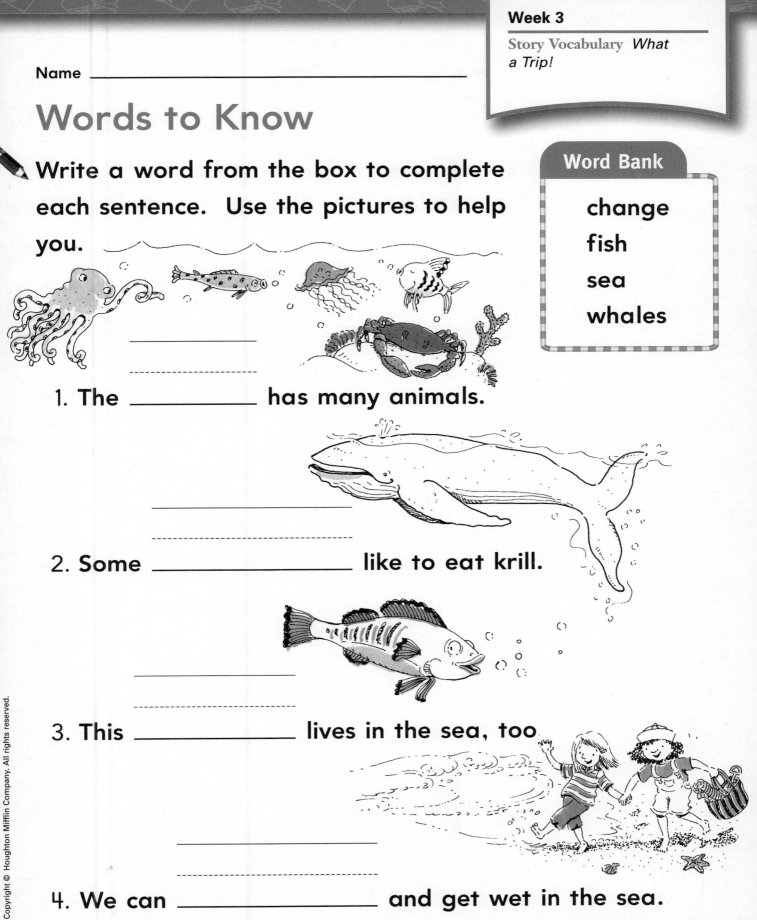

1. The _____ has many animals.

2. Some _____ like to eat krill.

3. This _____ lives in the sea, too

4. We can _____ and get wet in the sea.

Theme 3: **Let's Look Around!**　　137

Name _____

What Did You See?

Read each question. Cut out the pictures and sentences. Paste each picture and sentence next to the question it answers.

1. Where's the funny fish?

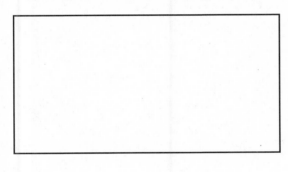

2. What can grab?

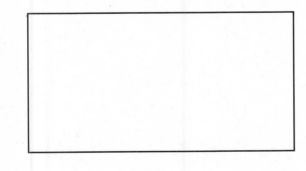

3. What can zig and zag?

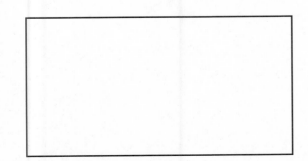

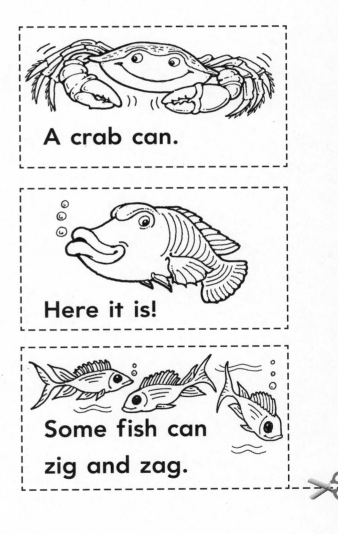

A crab can.

Here it is!

Some fish can zig and zag.

Theme 3: **Let's Look Around!**   **139**

Name _____

Spelling Spree

Add the letters. Write the Spelling Words.

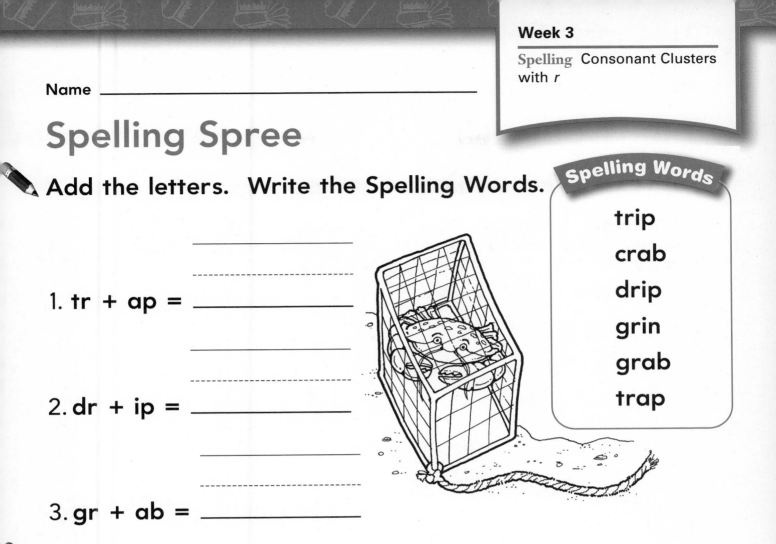

1. tr + ap = _____

_____

2. dr + ip = _____

_____

3. gr + ab = _____

Proofread each sentence. Circle each Spelling Word
that is wrong and write it correctly.

4. We go on a tirp. _____

5. We get a krab! _____

6. We grinn. _____

Spelling Words

trip
crab
drip
grin
grab
trap

Name _____

Plan Your Trip!

Write your ideas about your trip.

Where will you go?

_____

- - - - - - - - - - - - - - - - - -

_____

How will you get there?

_____

- - - - - - - - - - - - - - - - - -

_____

What will you do there?

_____

- - - - - - - - - - - - - - - - - -

_____

How will you get home?

_____

- - - - - - - - - - - - - - - - - -

_____

Name _____

Spelling Review

Each Spelling Word is missing one letter.
Write the missing letter.

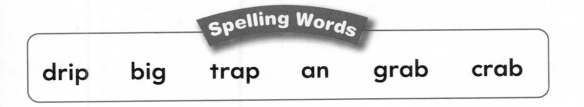

drip	big	trap	an	grab	crab

The missing letter is the first sound you hear

in _____ .

1. ____ n

The missing letter is the first sound you hear

in _____ .

2. b ____ g

Write two letters to complete each Spelling
Word.

3. _____ ab

4. _____ ap

5. _____ ab

6. _____ ip

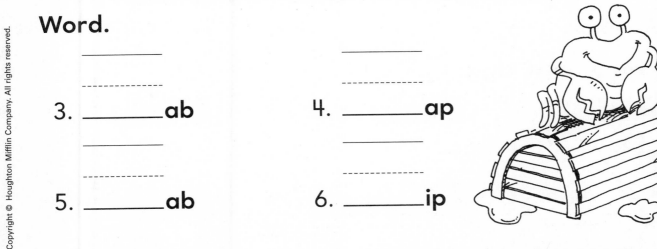

Theme 3: **Let's Look Around!**   **145**

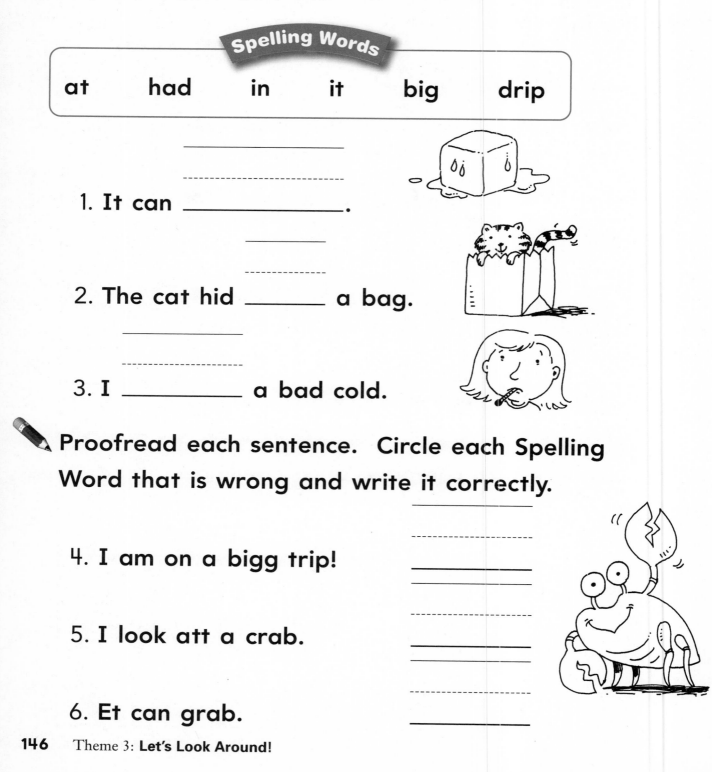

Name _____

Spelling Spree

Write a Spelling Word in each blank.

Spelling Words

at	had	in	it	big	drip

1. It can _____.

2. The cat hid _____ a bag.

3. I _____ a bad cold.

Proofread each sentence. Circle each Spelling Word that is wrong and write it correctly.

4. I am on a bigg trip!   _____

5. I look att a crab.   _____

6. Et can grab.   _____

Name _____

Words with Short *o*

Name each picture. Write **o** if the picture name has the short **o** sound.

1. _____

2. _____

3. _____

4. _____

5. _____

6. _____

7. _____

8. _____

9. _____

10. _____

11. _____

12. _____

13. _____

14. _____

15. _____

16. _____

Theme 4: **Family and Friends**   **147**

Name _____

Words with Short *o*

Read each sentence and circle the picture of the underlined word. Write the word.

1. <u>Dot</u> can pack for a trip.

_____

2. What is in the <u>box</u>?

_____

3. See Dot's <u>doll</u>.

_____

4. See Dot's <u>socks</u>.

_____

5. See Dot's <u>top</u>.

_____

Name _____

Clusters with *l*

Name each picture. Circle the letters that stand for the beginning sounds.

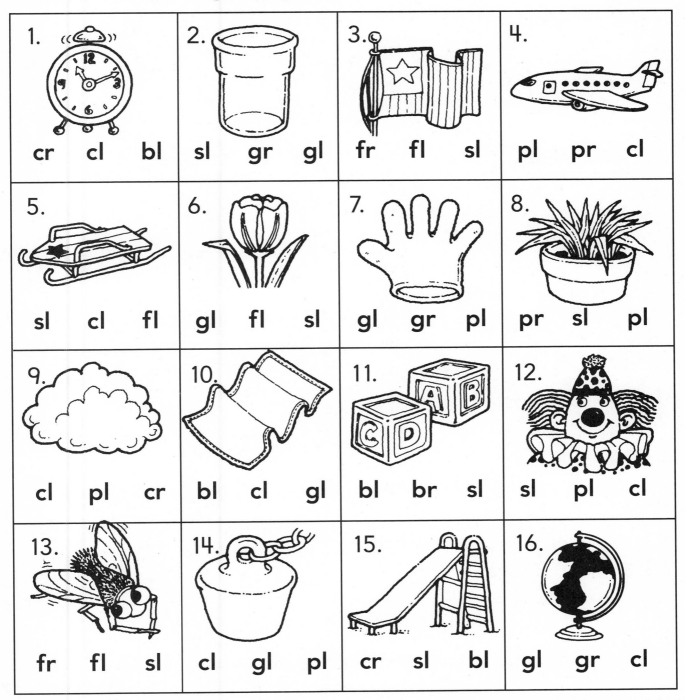

1. cr   cl   bl

2. sl   gr   gl

3. fr   fl   sl

4. pl   pr   cl

5. sl   cl   fl

6. gl   fl   sl

7. gl   gr   pl

8. pr   sl   pl

9. cl   pl   cr

10. bl   cl   gl

11. bl   br   sl

12. sl   pl   cl

13. fr   fl   sl

14. cl   gl   pl

15. cr   sl   bl

16. gl   gr   cl

Name _____

Clusters with *l*

Circle the word that names each picture.
Write the word.

1. flat
   flag

2. clock
   class

3. glass
   grass

4. block
   blot

5. plug
   slug

6. sled
   slacks

7. flap
   clap

8. flat
   flip

Draw a Conclusion

Read each set of sentences. Write your
conclusion.

1. Dan is cold.
   Dan sees a hat.

   _____

   Dan will _____

   _____

2. The vet looks at the pet.
   The pet is not sick.

   _____

   The pet will _____

   _____

Theme 4: **Family and Friends**   **151**

Words to Know

Write words from the box to complete the story.

Word Bank

| your | love | picture | children |

Come see the people in my family.

_____

Here is a _____.

We have a mother, a father, and two

_____

_____.

We all get lots of _____.

Who's in _____ family?

Name _____

Spelling Spree

Write the missing letters. Write the word.

Spelling Words

| on | not | got | box | hot | top |

1. h __ t _____

2. g __ t _____   3. n __ t _____

Proofread each sentence. Circle each Spelling Word that is wrong and write it correctly.

4. I have a big bocks. _____

5. Fran and I sit un it. _____

6. The tp falls in! _____

Theme 4: **Family and Friends**   **159**

What Is Your Answer?

Write a complete sentence to answer each question.

1. Who is in your family?

_____

_____

_____

_____

2. What fun does your family have?

_____

_____

_____

_____

Words with Short *e*

Name each picture. Write **e** if the picture
name has the short **e** sound.

1. _e_	2. ___	3. _e_	4. _e_
5. _e_	6. _e_	7. ___	8. _e_
9. _e_	10. ___	11. _e_	12. _e_
13. _e_	14. _e_	15. ___	16. _e_

Name _____

Words with Short *e*

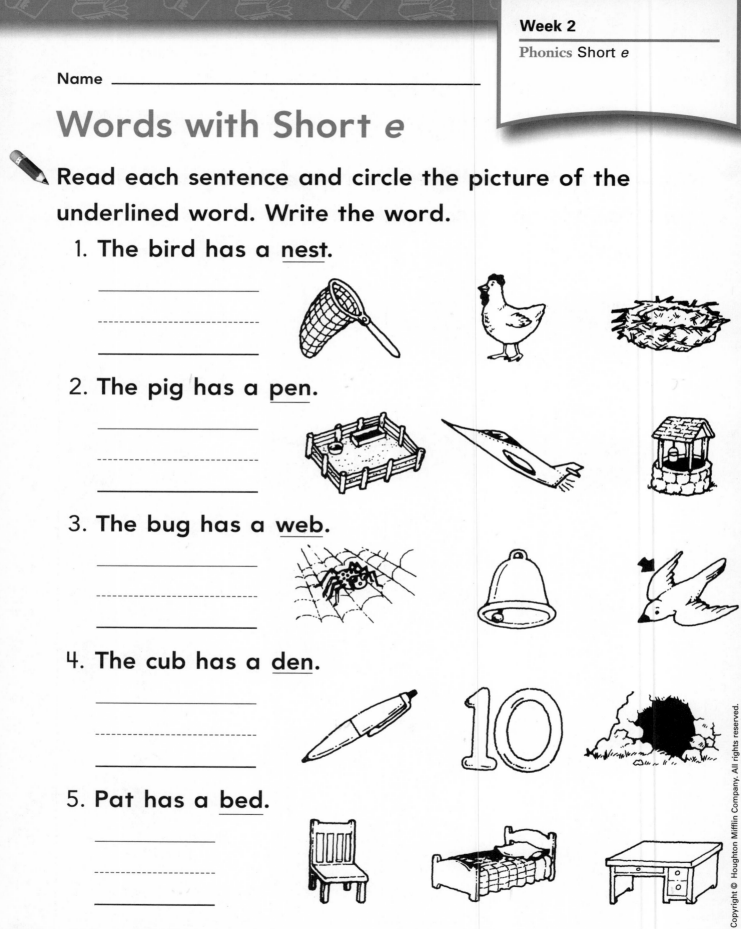

Read each sentence and circle the picture of the underlined word. Write the word.

1. **The bird has a <u>nest</u>.**

   _____

   - - - - - - - - - - - -

   _____

2. **The pig has a <u>pen</u>.**

   _____

   - - - - - - - - - - - -

   _____

3. **The bug has a <u>web</u>.**

   _____

   - - - - - - - - - - - -

   _____

4. **The cub has a <u>den</u>.**

   _____

   - - - - - - - - - - - -

   _____

5. **Pat has a <u>bed</u>.**

   _____

   - - - - - - - - - - - -

   _____

162 Theme 4: **Family and Friends**

Name _____

Clusters with *s*

Name each picture. Circle the letters that stand for the beginning sounds.

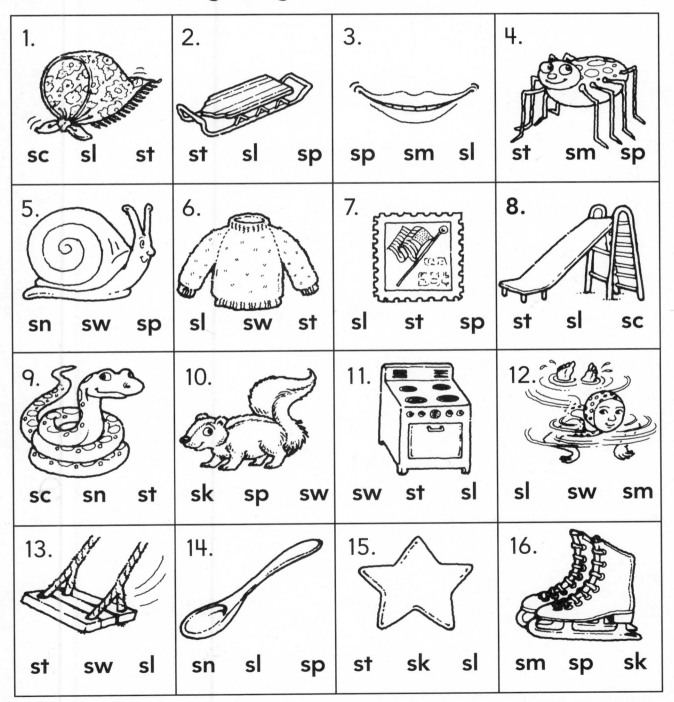

1. sc sl **st**	2. **st** sl sp	3. sp **sm** sl	4. st sm **sp**
5. **sn** sw sp	6. sl **sw** st	7. sl **st** sp	8. st **sl** sc
9. **sc** sn st	10. **sk** sp sw	11. **sw** st sl	12. sl **sw** sm
13. st sw **sl**	14. sn sl **sp**	15. **st** sk sl	16. sm sp **sk**

Theme 4: **Family and Friends**   **163**

Name _____

Clusters with *s*

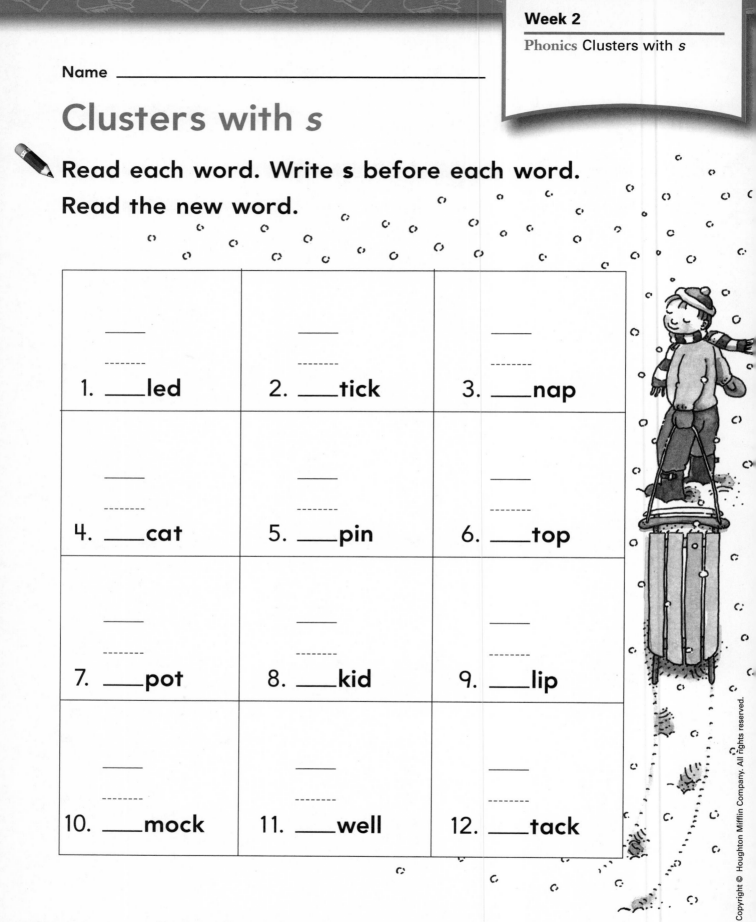

Read each word. Write **s** before each word.
Read the new word.

1. ___**led**	2. ___**tick**	3. ___**nap**
4. ___**cat**	5. ___**pin**	6. ___**top**
7. ___**pot**	8. ___**kid**	9. ___**lip**
10. ___**mock**	11. ___**well**	12. ___**tack**

Name _____

Words to Know

Write words from the box to complete the story.

Word Bank

| sing | read | today | play |

Fran is my best girl friend.

She can _____ like a bird.

She can _____ tricks too.

I will write to Fran _____ .
I will tell my best friend what I did.

I know Fran will write back.

I can _____ what she did too!

Name _____

The Big Day!

Read the story. Draw a picture to go with it.

One day there is a sign at the door.

First Prize for Best  Picture

Jack got a picture of a boy and his dog.

Jack got first prize and everyone smiled.

Name _____

Write About It!

Choose a topic. Then write some sentences about it.

Topic:

_____
- -
_____
- -
_____

Sentences:

_____
- -
_____
- -
_____
- -
_____
- -
_____
- -
_____

Name _____

Words with Short *u*

Write **u** to complete each word. Then write
two of the words to complete the sentence.

1. b__s

2. f__n

3. d__ck

4. dr__m

5. t__b

6. j__st

7. The _____ swims in the _____ .

Name _____

Words with Short *u*

Read the word in dark print. Circle and write
the rhyming word in the box.

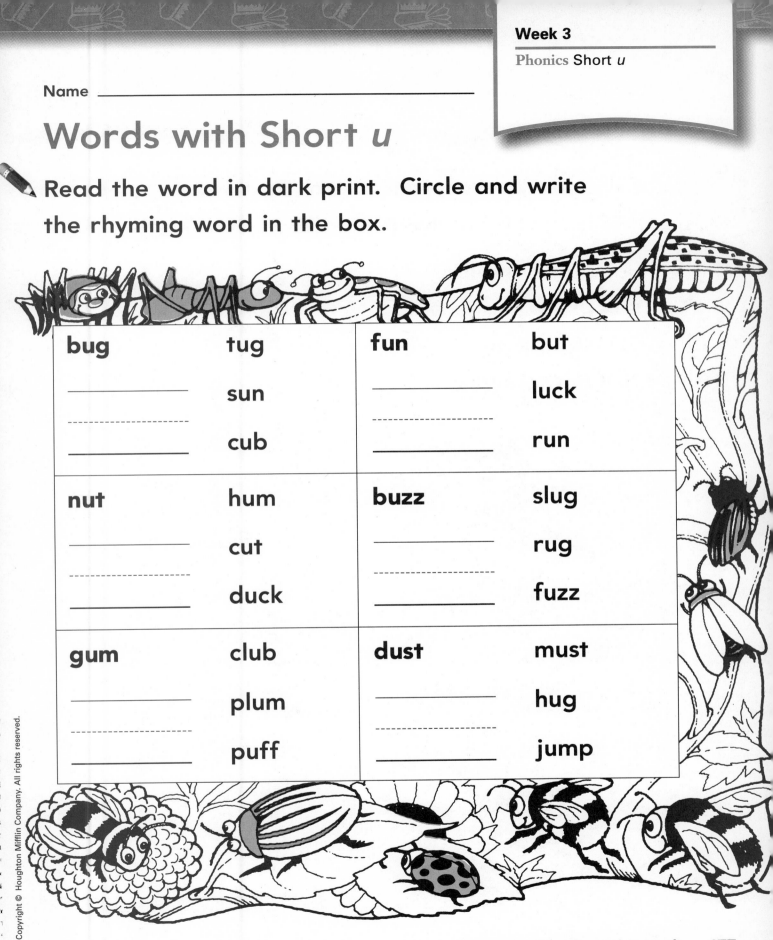

bug	tug
_____	sun
----------	cub

fun	but
_____	luck
----------	run

nut	hum
_____	cut
----------	duck

buzz	slug
_____	rug
----------	fuzz

gum	club
_____	plum
----------	puff

dust	must
_____	hug
----------	jump

Name _____

Triple Clusters

Read the story. Write each word in dark print next to the picture it names.

Big Gus **splits** the logs.
The **scraps** go in the bin.
Big Gus **scrubs** up.
He **strums** and hums.

1. _____

2. _____

3. _____

4. _____

Name _____

Words to Know

Write words from the box to complete the story.

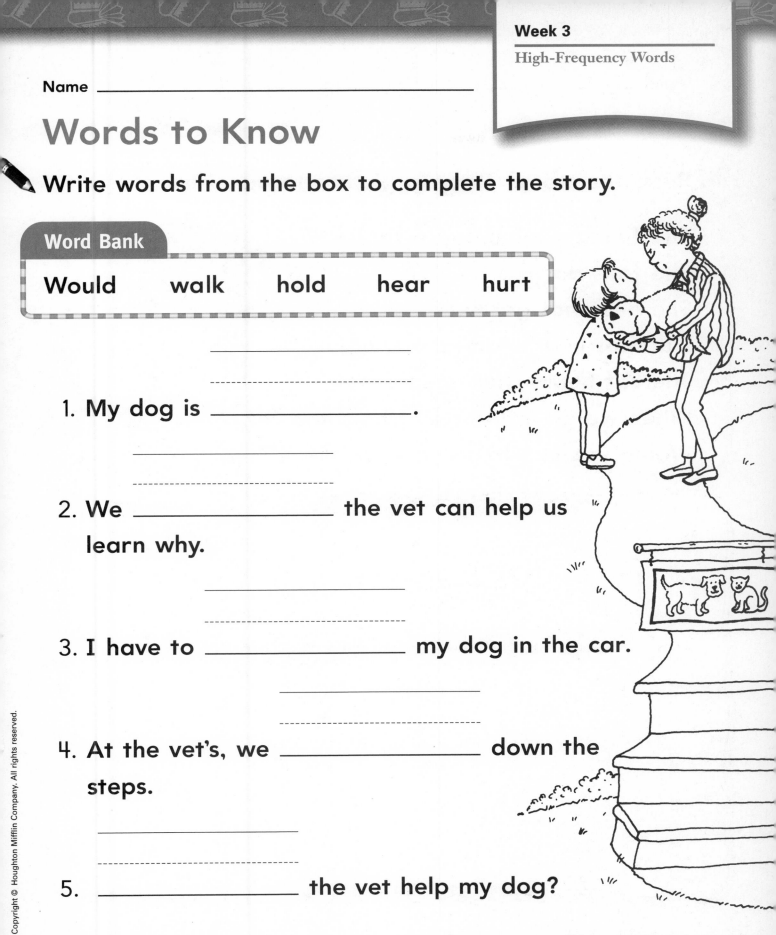

Word Bank

| Would | walk | hold | hear | hurt |

1. My dog is _____ .

2. We _____ the vet can help us learn why.

3. I have to _____ my dog in the car.

4. At the vet's, we _____ down the steps.

5. _____ the vet help my dog?

Name _____

Words to Know

Read the story. Draw a picture to go with it.

The funny cat can learn to walk.

She falls down.

She does not get hurt.

I do not hear Mom and Dad.

The cat hears their steps.

When we go in the car, I hold the cat.

Would you like to see the cat?

At the Pet Shop

Circle the word that completes each sentence.
Write the word.

_____

1. Judd felt glad his big _____ had come!

   day   down

2. He and Dad walked to the pet _____.

   step   shop

3. "The _____ are we get one pup," said Dad.

   read   rules

4. "I hear a _____," said Judd. "What a pup!"

   noise   nose

What's Happening?

 Read each sentence and look at the pictures. Circle and color the picture that shows what happens in the story.

1. **Bud is Ben's pet.**

2. **Ben and Mom look here for Bud.**

3. **Ben and Mom find Bud here.**

Write what happens at the end of the story.

_____

- - - - - - - - - - - - - - - - - - - -

_____

- - - - - - - - - - - - - - - - - - - -

_____

The Short *u* Sound

✏ **Read each clue. Write the Spelling Word.**

Spelling Words

up	us	but	fun	cut	run

1. **not walk:**

_____

2. **not down:**

_____

3. **like we:**

_____

4. **what tricks are:**

_____

✏ **Write the two words that rhyme with hut.**

5. _____

6. _____

Name _____

Where's the Question?

Read each group of words. Underline each asking sentence.

1. The class play is today.

   What day is it?

2. Who is in the play?

   The play has animals.

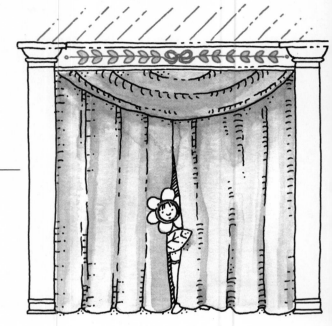

3. Can we go to the play?

   I can write a play.

4. The play is fun.

   Where is the next play?

Name _____

Spelling Spree

Write the letter for each shape. Make Spelling Words.

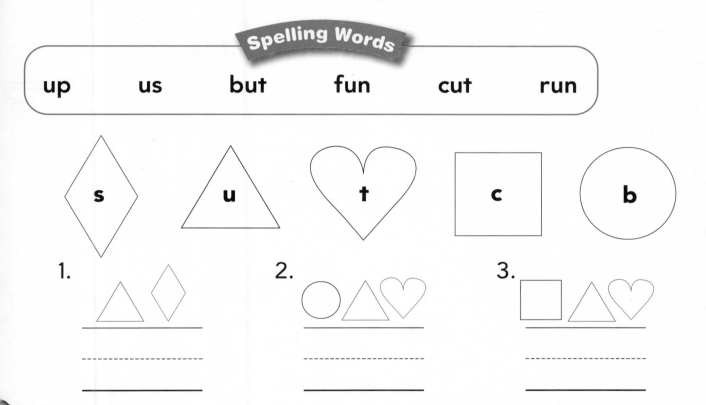

Spelling Words

| up | us | but | fun | cut | run |

1. _____

2. _____

3. _____

Proofread each sentence. Circle each Spelling Word
that is wrong and write it correctly.

_____

4. I like to runn.

_____

5. It is a lot of fon.

_____

6. I can run ub a hill.

Name _____

What's Your Question?

Write questions for each question word.

_____

1. Who _____

2. What _____

3. Where _____

4. Why _____

Name _____

Spelling Review

Write a Spelling Word next to each number.

Spelling Words

| on | yes | box | ten | but | fun |

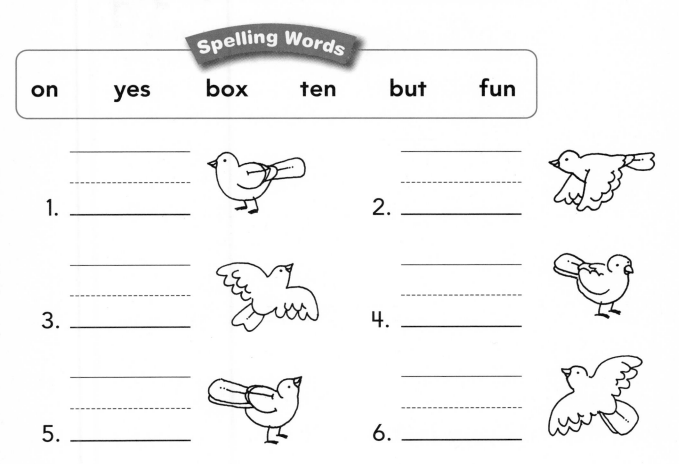

1. _____

2. _____

3. _____

4. _____

5. _____

6. _____

Which words have the short *e* sound?
Color those birds red.
Which words have the short *u* sound?
Color those birds blue.
Which words have the short *o* sound?
Color those birds brown.

Name _____

Spelling Spree

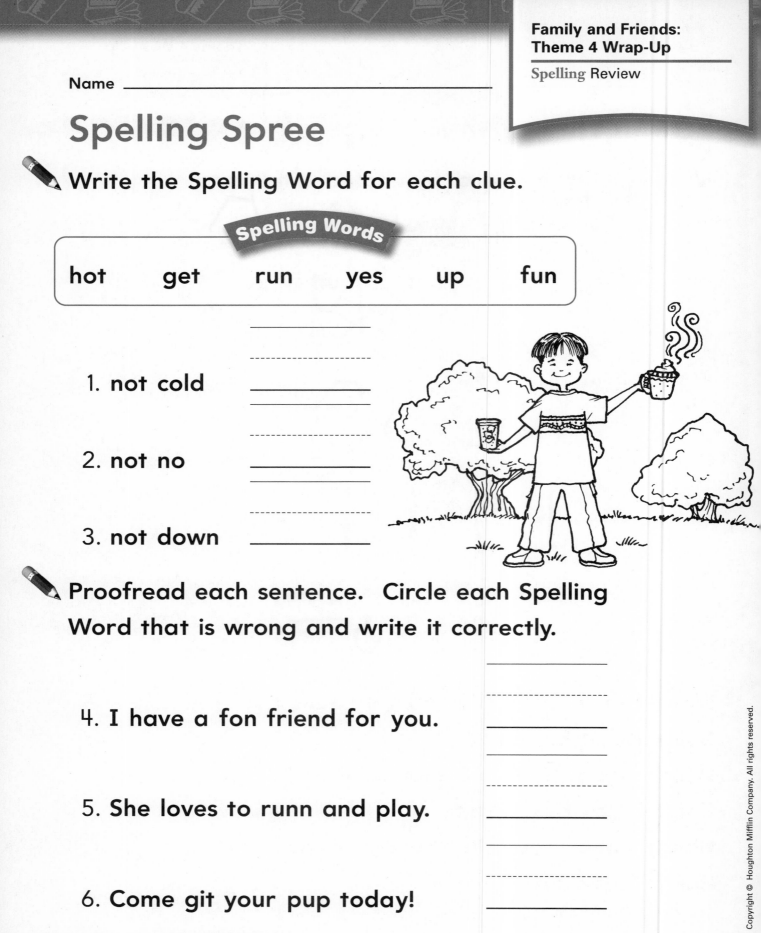

Write the Spelling Word for each clue.

Spelling Words

| hot | get | run | yes | up | fun |

1. not cold _____

2. not no _____

3. not down _____

Proofread each sentence. Circle each Spelling Word that is wrong and write it correctly.

4. I have a fon friend for you. _____

5. She loves to runn and play. _____

6. Come git your pup today! _____

My Handbook

Contents

Andy Apple

Benny Bear

Callie Cat

Dudley Duck

Edna Elephant

Fifi Fish

Gertie Goose

Hattie Horse

Iggy Iguana

Jumping Jill

Keely Kangaroo

Larry Lion

Mimi Mouse

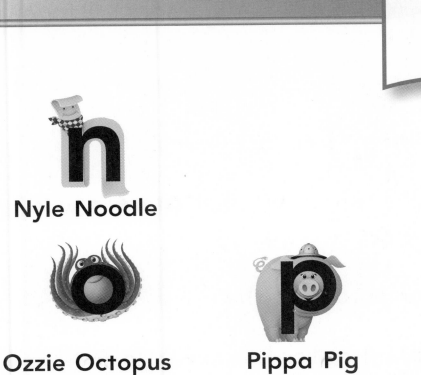

Nyle Noodle

Ozzie Octopus

Pippa Pig

Queenie Queen

Reggie Rooster

Sammy Seal

Tiggy Tiger

Umbie Umbrella

Vinny Volcano

Willy Worm

Mr. X-Ray

Yetta Yo-Yo

Zelda Zebra

1. Look at the letters from left to right.

2. Think about the sounds for the letters, and look for word parts you know.

3. Blend the sounds to read the word.

4. Ask yourself: Is it a word I know? Does it make sense in what I am reading?

5. If not, ask yourself: What else can I try?

Predict/Infer

► Think about the title, the illustrations, and what you have read so far.

► Tell what you think will happen next or what you will learn.

Question

► Ask yourself questions as you read.

Monitor/Clarify

► Ask yourself if what you are reading makes sense.

► If you don't understand something, reread, read ahead, or use the illustrations.

Summarize

► Think about the main ideas or the important parts of the story.

► Tell the important things in your own words.

Evaluate

► Ask yourself: Do I like what I have read? Am I learning what I wanted to know?

Trace and write the letters.

Aa Aa Aa Aa Aa

Bb Bb Bb

Cc Cc Cc Cc Cc

Dd Dd Dd Dd

Ee Ee Ee

Ff Ff

Gg Gg

Trace and write the letters.

Hh Hh

Ii Ii

Jj Jj

Kk Kk

Ll Ll

Mm Mm

Trace and write the letters.

Nn Nn

Oo Oo

Pp Pp

Qq Qq

Rr Rr

Ss Ss

Tt Tt

Trace and write the letters.

Uu Uu

Vv Vv

Ww Ww

Xx Xx

Yy Yy

Zz Zz

Trace and write the letters.

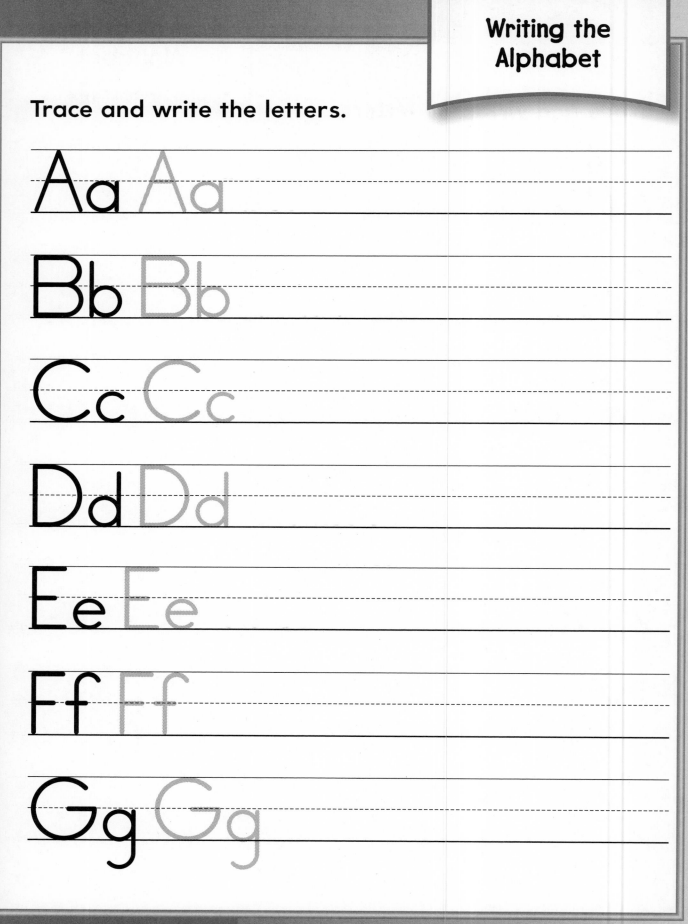

Aa Aa

Bb Bb

Cc Cc

Dd Dd

Ee Ee

Ff Ff

Gg Gg

Trace and write the letters.

Hh Hh

Ii Ii

Jj Jj

Kk Kk

Ll Ll

Mm Mm

Trace and write the letters.

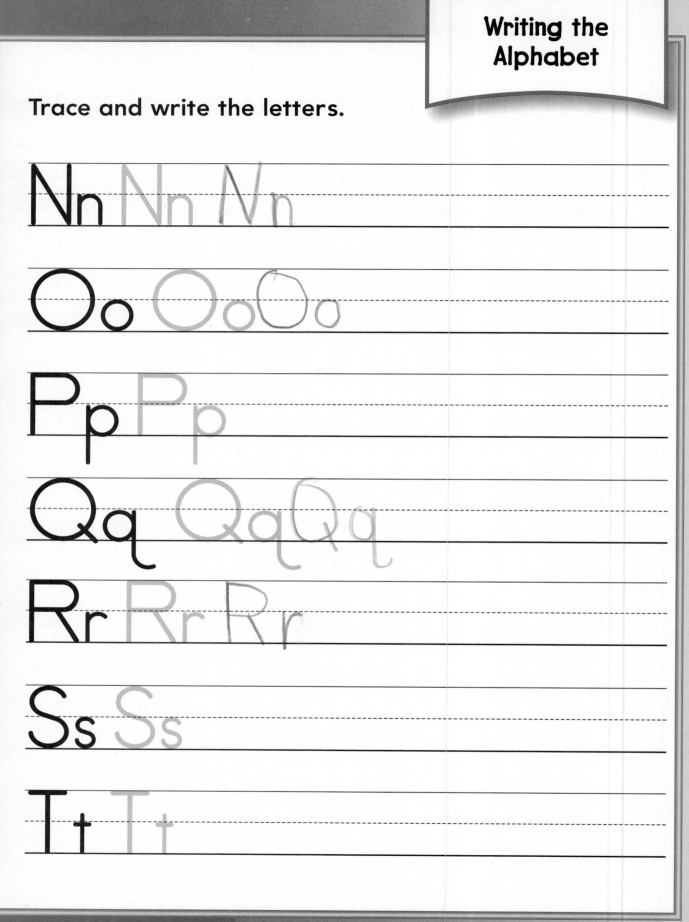

Trace and write the letters.

U u U u

V v V v

W w W w

X x X x

Y y Y y

Z z Z z

How to Study a Word

1. **LOOK** at the word.

2. **SAY** the word.

3. **THINK** about the word.

4. **WRITE** the word.

5. **CHECK** the spelling.

A
a
about
again
always
and
any
around
as

B
back
because
before

C
cannot
come
coming
could

D
do
down

F
for
friend
from

G
getting
goes
going

H
has
have
her
here
his
house
how

I
I
if
into
is

L
little

M
many
more

N
never
new
now

O

of

one

or

other

our

out

over

P

people

R

right

S

said

some

T

than

the

their

there

they

thing

to

tried

two

V

very

W

want

was

were

what

when

where

who

would

Y

you

your

Mr. C's Dinner

The Short _i_ sound

in

it

him

Spelling Words

1. in
2. it
3. him
4. big
5. sit
6. did

Challenge Words

1. dish
2. milk

My Study List
Add your own
spelling words
on the back. ➡

Seasons

The Short _a_ sound

an

at

can

Spelling Words

1. an
2. at
3. can
4. cat
5. had
6. man

Challenge Words

1. catch
2. add

My Study List
Add your own
spelling words
on the back. ➡

Name_____

My Study List

_____

1. _____

2. _____

3. _____

4. _____

5. _____

6. _____

Name_____

My Study List

_____

1. _____

2. _____

3. _____

4. _____

5. _____

6. _____

Let's Look Around!
Spelling Review

Spelling Words

1. an
2. in
3. trap
4. at
5. it
6. crab
7. had
8. big
9. drip
10. grab

See the back for Challenge Words.

My Study List
Add your own spelling words on the back. ➡

What a Trip!

Consonant Clusters with *r*	
trip	crab
drip	grin

Spelling Words

1. trip
2. crab
3. drip
4. grin
5. grab
6. trap

Challenge Words

1. crack
2. brown

My Study List
Add your own spelling words on the back. ➡

Name _____

My Study List

_____

1. _____

2. _____

3. _____

4. _____

5. _____

6. _____

Name _____

My Study List

_____

1. _____

2. _____

3. _____

4. _____

5. _____

6. _____

Challenge Words

1. add
2. dish
3. crack

The Best Pet

The Short _e_ sound

get

ten

red

Spelling Words

1. get
2. ten
3. red
4. pet
5. men
6. yes

Challenge Words

1. tent
2. bell

My Study List
Add your own
spelling words
on the back. ➡

Who's in a Family?

The Short _o_ sound

on

not

box

Spelling Words

1. on
2. not
3. got
4. box
5. hot
6. top

Challenge Words

1. pond
2. doll

My Study List
Add your own
spelling words
on the back. ➡

Name_____

My Study List

1. _____

2. _____

3. _____

4. _____

5. _____

6. _____

Name_____

My Study List

1. _____

2. _____

3. _____

4. _____

5. _____

6. _____

Family and Friends
Spelling Review

Spelling Words

1. on
2. get
3. up
4. hot
5. ten
6. but
7. box
8. fun
9. yes
10. run

See the back for Challenge Words.

My Study List
Add your own spelling words on the back. ➡

Bud's Day Out

The Short _u_ sound
up
us
but

Spelling Words

1. up
2. us
3. but
4. fun
5. cut
6. run

Challenge Words

1. jump
2. plum

My Study List
Add your own spelling words on the back. ➡

Name _____

My Study List

_____

1. _____

2. _____

3. _____

4. _____

5. _____

6. _____

Name _____

My Study List

_____

1. _____

2. _____

3. _____

4. _____

5. _____

6. _____

Challenge Words

1. pond
2. bell
3. plum

A A A A B B C C D D

E E E F F G G H H

I I J J K K L L M

M N N O O P P Q Q

R R S S T T U U V

V W W X X Y Y Z Z

You can add punctuation marks or other letters to the blanks.
Letter Tray
⬇

Letter Tray
c a t

fold

fold

fold

d	d	c	c	b	b	a	a	a
h	h	g	g	f	f	e	e	e
m	l	l	k	k	j	j	i	i
q	q	p	p	o	o	n	n	m
v	u	u	t	t	s	s	r	r
z	z	y	y	x	x	w	w	v

fold

fold

fold

Theme 1, Week 3	Theme 1, Week 2	Theme 1, Week 1
a	and	go
find	here	on
have	jump	the
one	not	
to	too	
who	we	

Theme 1, Week 3	Theme 1, Week 2	Theme 1, Week 1

You can add your own words for sentence building.

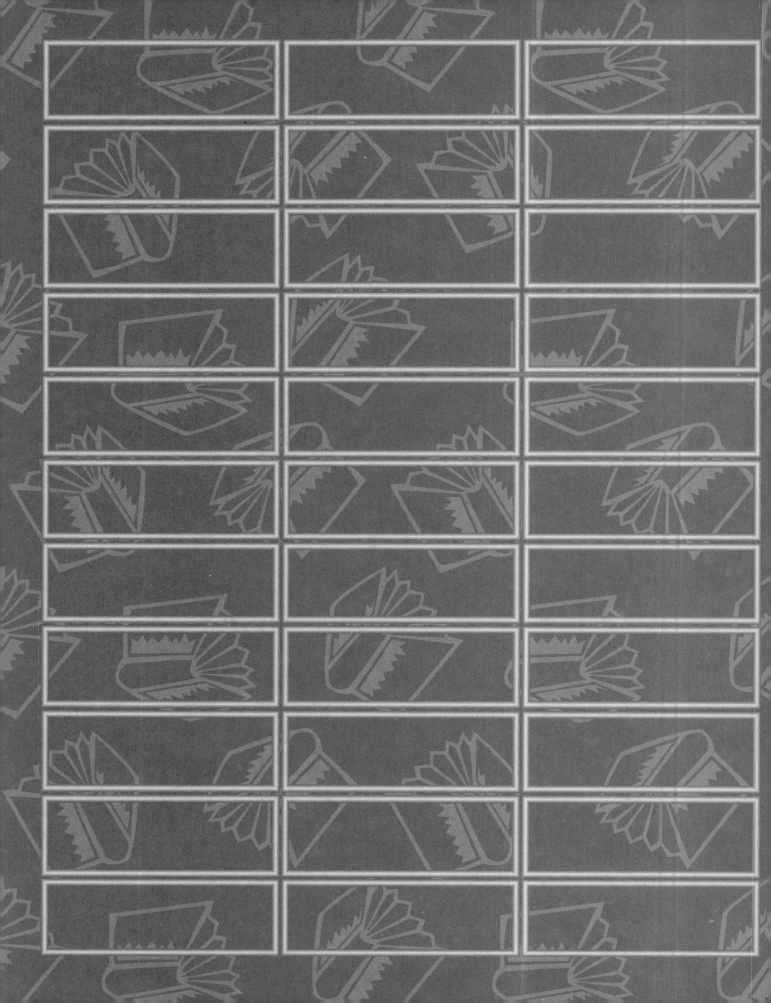

Theme 2, Week 3	Theme 2, Week 2	Theme 2, Week 1
are	do	five
away	for	four
does	is	in
he	me	once
live	my	three
pull	said	two
they	you	upon
where	I	what

You can add your own words for sentence building.

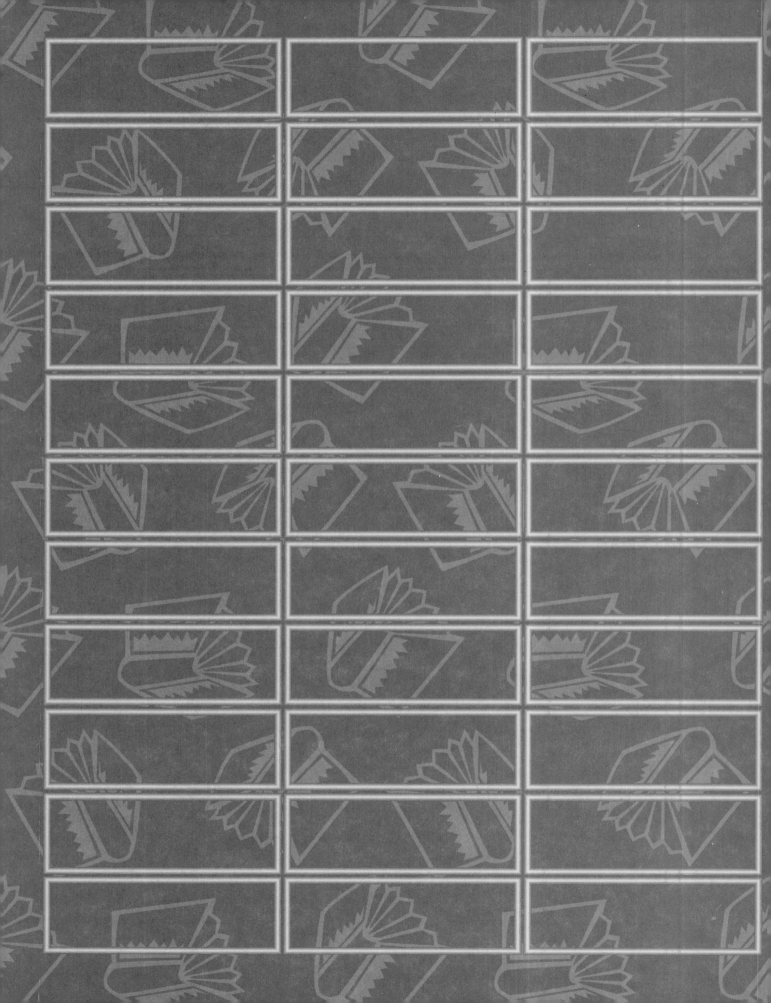

Theme 3, Week 3	Theme 3, Week 2	Theme 3, Week 1
also	all	animal
blue	call	bird
brown	eat	cold
color	every	fall
funny	first	flower
green	never	full
like	paper	look
many	shall	of
some	why	see
Theme 3, Week 3	Theme 3, Week 2	Theme 3, Week 1

You can add your own words for sentence building.

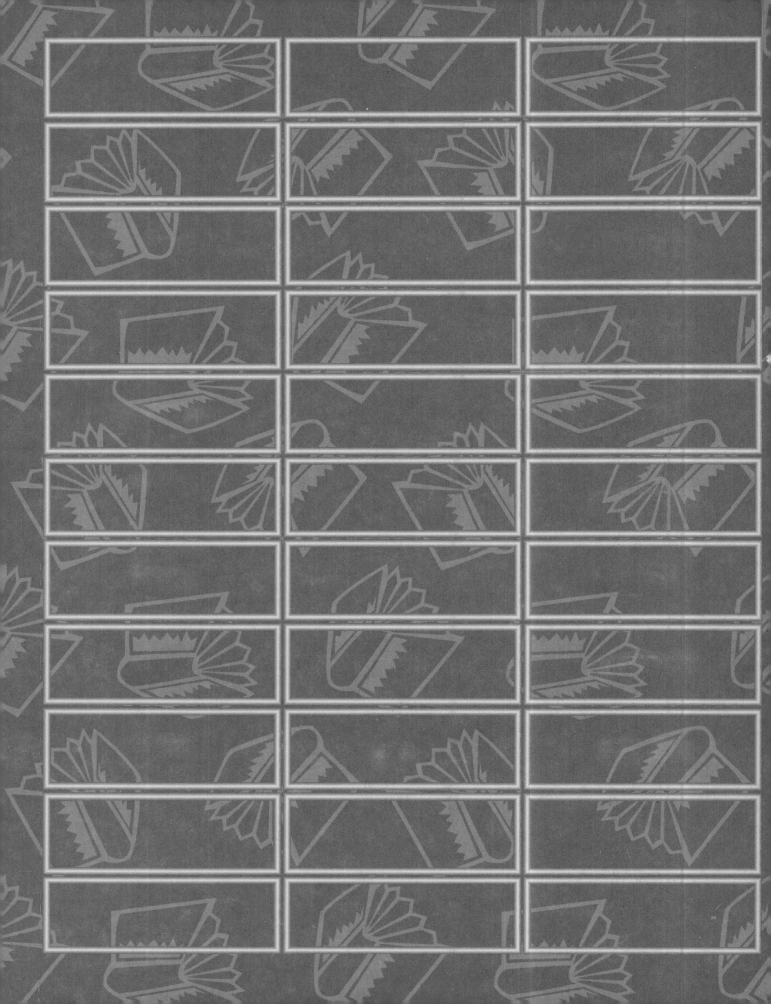

Theme 4, Week 3	Theme 4, Week 2	Theme 4, Week 1
car	play	come
down	friend	children
walk	girl	family
hear	she	father
hold	read	love
hurt	sing	mother
learn	today	people
their	write	picture
would	know	your

You can add your own words for sentence building.

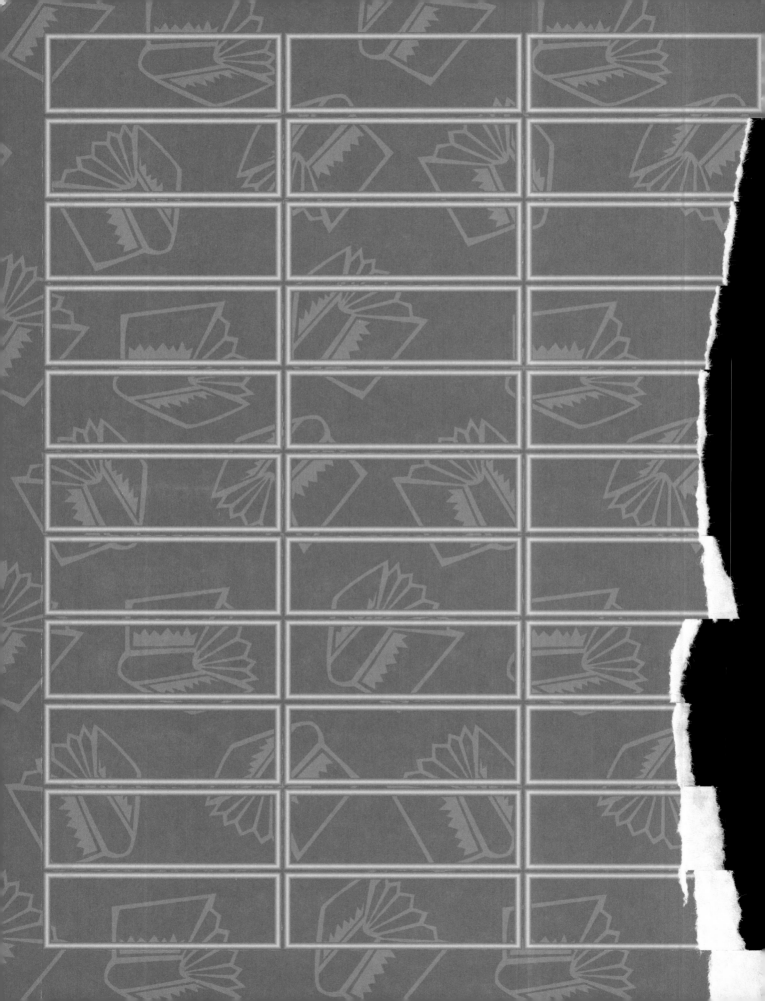